How I Saw It

PAT:

THANKS FOR KEEPING THE TRADITION ALIVE! PLUS THANKS FOR BEING A DERBY FRIEND; YOU HAVE A THE BEST DEALERSHIP ON STATE Rd. KEEP ON COASTING!

THANKS,
Jeff Iula
"MR. DERBY"
9/20/11

How I Saw It

My Photographic Memory of the Soap Box Derby

Jeff Iula and Bill Ignizio
Carol Slatter, Researcher and Photo Editor
Tom Bacher, Content Editor

RINGTAW BOOKS
AKRON, OHIO

Copyright © 2011 by Jeff Iula and Bill Ignizio

All rights reserved • First Edition 2011 • Manufactured in the United States of America • All inquiries and permission requests should be addressed to the Publisher, The University of Akron Press, Akron, Ohio 44325-1703.

15 14 13 12 11   5 4 3 2 1

ISBN 978-1-935603-07-8 (paperback)
LCCN 2011929626

The paper used in this publication meets the minimum requirements of American National Standard for Information Sciences—Permanence of Paper for Printed Library Materials, ANSI z39.48–1984. ∞

Cover and interior design by Zac Bettendorf. Cover and title page photo by Nancy Iula, used with permission.

Contents

List of Illustrations vi
Acknowledgments x
Introduction 1

1930s   The Beginning 3

1940s   A Great Start 17

1950s   Seasoned Champions 27

1960s   Hey Days 39

1970s   A Changing Time 51

1980s   Family Traditions 67

1990s   Enduring Legacy 75

2000s   The Need for Tradition 85

2010s   Today's Race 95

Cars 99

Memorabilia 108

How I Saw It 115

List of Illustrations

Myron Scott[a]	1
Randy Custer[h]	4
Dayton Daily News Entry Form	5A
Dayton Race	5B
Dayton Daily News article[h]	5C
1933 winners[h]	6A
Randy Custer[h]	6B
Myron Scott[h]	6C
Close finish[h]	6D
Bob Gravett & Old No. 7[h]	6E
A heat start[h]	6F
Derby pits[m]	7A
Helmet factory[b]	7B
Promotional car[j]	7C
Sledding at Derby Downs[a]	8A
Derby Downs construction[j]	8B
Aerial view of Derby Downs[j]	8C
Robert Turner[j]	9A
Bob Gravett & Old No. 7[n]	9B
First heat[m]	9C
Dayton Daily News[h]	10
Australian race[d]	11A
South African race	11B
Graham McNamee[j]	12
Final heat[a]	13A
Wreck[a]	13B
All-American Banquet	13C
Paul Brown[j]	13D
Dick Ballard[j]	14
Bob Berger[j]	15A
Bob Ballard[j]	15B
Overbey, Scott, Fulton, & Schlemmer[j]	18A
Wilbur Shaw & Tommy Fisher[j]	18B
Bill Zoller	18C
First live TV broadcast	18D
Derby founders[a]	18E
All-American Awards Show[j]	19A
Pre-race parade	19B
Camp Y-Noah[j]	19C
Race day[j]	19D
World Champions[j]	19E
Letter from Chevrolet	20
George Burns & Gracie Allen[j]	21A
Derks, Muhl, & Klepsch[j]	21B
Starting line[j]	21C
Claude Smith	22
Tom Fisher[j]	23A
Harold Hayes	23B
Leo Osterman[j]	23C
Fred Derks[j]	23D
Gil Klecan[j]	24, 25A & B
Parade of Champions[j]	28A
Shepherd, Thomas, & Lunn[a]	28B
Letter from President Eisenhower	28C
Wheel factory[j]	28D
Doupe & Hancock crash[a]	29A
Terry Townsend[a]	29B
Abbott & Costello[j]	30
Oil Can Race[j]	31A
Celebrities[j]	31B, C
Joey Lunn & celebrities[a]	31D
Celebrities[j]	32A
Andy Devine[j]	32B
Richard Nixon	33A
Barney Townsend	33B
Celebrities[j]	33C
Darwin Cooper & celebrities[j]	33D
Wilbur Shaw & Clark Gable	33E
Freddy Mohler[j]	34
Terry Townsend[j]	35A
Dick Kemp[a]	35B
Celebrities[j]	35C
Kenneth Johnson[j]	35D
Derby staff & volunteers[j]	36A
Derby Downs[j]	36B
Jim Miley	37A
Peter Christlief[j]	37B
Planning the 19th race[j]	37C
Welcoming Ceremonies[j]	37D
Herb Alpert	40A
Oil Can Race[a]	40B
Kenny Cline	40C
David Mann[j]	40D
29th All-American trophies[j]	40E
Weigh station[a]	41A
Simpson & Peters wreck[a]	41B
Teruo Hanashiro[a]	41C
Final heat, 1969[a]	41D
Terry Lesko[a]	41E
Jeff Iula[a]	42
Letter from President Kennedy	43A
Robert Russell Bennett[j]	43B
Jeff Iula	43C
Letter from President Johnson	43D
Oil Can Race[a]	44A
Downtown Akron Parade[j]	44B
Oil Can Race	45A, C
David Canary	45B
Dick York	45D
Parade[a]	46
John McDaniels Jr.[j]	47A
Celebrities[a]	47B
Lutz Aderhold[a]	47C
Bob Logan[j]	47D
Judy Carne[j]	47E
Branch Lew[j]	47F
Derby banquet[j]	48
Bobby Kennedy[j]	49A
Celebrities[j]	49B
Fans on race day	49C & D
Kelly Jr., Bell, & Dunaway[j]	49E

vi   *How I Saw It*

Chuck Ayers Illustration[f]	52, 53B
Nancy Eichenlaub	53A
Joe Murphy[a]	53C
Craig Kitchen	54
Art Arfons	55A
Akron Area Chamber of Commerce	55B
Larry Blair[a]	55C
First dead heat[o]	55D
Ron Reed	55E
Zanesville crash[o]	56, 57
Karren Stead	58
Chevrolet quits Derby[a]	59A
Novar Electronics becomes sponsor[a]	59B
Letter from Chevrolet	59C
Parade of Corvettes[a]	60
Novar Electronics[o]	61A
Joey Lunn	61B
Peel, Underwood, & Ford	61C
Russ Yurk	61D
Chris Noyes	62A
National Derby Rallies	62B
Phil Raber	63A & B
Three car wreck	63C
Chevrolet[s]	63D
James Gronen	64A[o], B
Richard Decatur	65A
Timothy Sean McNeil	65B
Allen Walker[a]	65C
Joey Lunn & Scott Baio[g]	68
Parachutist Pat Kane[g]	69
Bob Turner[k]	70
Dale Earnhardt Sr.	71A
50th anniversary[g]	71B
Christopher Roberts	71C
Jeff Iula & Ron Baker	71D
Aerial view of Derby Downs[r]	72
Carol Anne Sullivan[o]	73A

Past world champions & celebrities[g]	73B
Burdgick, Hanks, & Koch[g]	73C
Anita Jackson & celebrities[g]	73D
Kelly Dughi[g]	76
Bob Turner	77A
Heather Seabeck	77B
Garcia & Medlock crash[o]	77C
Midas breaking area	77D
Indy rookie & champions[g]	77E
Ross Mallinger & celebrities	77F
First National Bank	78
Teresa Oles	79A
Super Kids Classic	79B
Celebrity luncheon[g]	79C
Champs reunite	79D
Oil Can Race	79E
Myron Scott & Jeff Iula	80
Ralph & Jeff Iula[g]	81A
Loris & Bob Troyer	81B
Kelly Dughi[g]	81C
Letter from President Ford	81D
Danielle Del Ferraro	82
Sami Jones	83A
Jeff Iula & Jon Provost	83B
James Marsh	83C
Loren Hurst[g]	83D
Indy 500 museum	86
Rally World Champions	87A
Derby Downs	87B
Ron Reed	88
Parade of Champions[g]	89A
Tony Deluca & Jeff Iula[g]	89B
Mason Bell & Jeff Iula	89C
Cars on display	89D
Reunion[g]	89E
Bob Troyer & Jeff Iula[g]	90
Future champs on parade[g]	91A

Megan Evans[g]	91B
Motorcycles on parade	91C
Home Depot[g]	92
Ducky Downs & the Kubick family	93A
Jeff Iula & Tyler Gallagher	93B
Letter from President Bush	93C
Goodyear	93D
Nathan Gamble[l]	96A
Dennis VanFossen & Nathan Gamble[p]	96B
Corbin Bernsen[p]	96C, 97A
Ralph Waite & Derby fans[p]	97B
Jeff Iula[p]	97C
Nathan Gamble[p]	98A, B, C
25Hill scene[p]	98D
Moosbrugger & Litherland	100A
1934 race	100B
Jack Furstenberg[j]	100C
Hansen, Kline, & Mossiman[j]	100D
Indianapolis local race, 1935	100E
John Tabor[m]	101A
Jack Thompson[j]	101B
Robert Holland[j]	101C
Walter Johnson[j]	101D
Louis Adams[j]	101E
Herbert Herrmann[j]	102A
Cliff Hardesty[j]	102B
Miley, Hilligoss, & Ashley[j]	102C
Douglas Falcon	102D
Barney Townsend	103A
Jim Kordon	103B
Vince Rubino	103C
Kirk Murphy	104A
Cleveland local race, 1967	104B
Kenny Cline	104C
David West	104D
Michael Cobb	104E
Quentin Thomas	105A

How I Saw It   vii

Marion F. Cauhape 105B
Ken Underwood 105C
Billy Ford 105D
Kim Kirby 106A
Joseph Frank Tully 106B
Dale Wallace Brainard 106C
Derek Fitzgerald 106D
Jeff Townsend 107A
Steve Frechino 107B
Bruce Schlegel 107C
Stuart Paul 107D
Purol, Frye, & Jones[g] 107E
Zak Boll[g] 107F
USA Today insert[q] 112A
Derby pennant 112B
Ad from *Boys' Life*[j] 112C
"Sixty years at Derby Downs"[a] 112D
Akron Beacon Journal insert[a] 113
60th anniversary poster[c] 114A
Movie poster[t] 114B
Jeff & Ralph Iula[g] 115
Jeff Iula, Billy Ford, & Jay Iula[e] 116A
Jeff Iula & Bob Baynes 116B
Nancy & Jeff Iula[g] 116C
Jeff & Nancy Iula's wedding party[o] 116D
Chris Roberts & Jeff Iula 116E
Jerri Roberts & family 117A
Kelly Dughi 117B
Carrie Cole 117C
Trinity Kubick 117D
Jeff Iula & Dick Goddard 117E
Jeff & Ralph Iula 118A
Letter from Myron Scott 118B
Jeff Iula & Corbin Bersen 118C

Illustrations courtesy of
[a] *Akron Beacon Journal*
[b] Albert Backlund
[c] All-American Soap Box Derby
[d] Australian Press Bureau
[e] Bill Ford
[f] Chuck Ayers
[g] Daniel Mainzer
[h] *Dayton Daily News*
[i] Firestone
[j] General Motors
[k] Joe Stair
[l] Kelleigh Miller
[m] R. R. McCreary Studio
[n] Myron Scott
[o] Richard Acker
[p] Todd Biss Photography
[q] *USA Today*
[r] Wayne Alley
[s] W. J. Wolf
[t] WVIZ/PBS ideastream© & Bridgestone Corporation

All other illustrations are from unknown sources.

In Memory of Ralph Iula

Acknowledgements

We wish to thank our wives, Nancy Iula and Sandi Ignizio, for all their help with this project. We also wish to thank Rick Acker, Chuck Ayers, Ron Baker, Mason Bell, Corbin Bernsen, Carol Biliczky, Mary Ellen Boll, Merle Boll, Bruce Buchholzer, R. G. Canning, Lynne Collier, Kenny Cline, Harrison Criss, Tony DeLuca, Bob Earley, Jack Engelke, Millie Esque, Shirley Evans, Tex Finsterwald, Derek Fitzgerald, Billy Ford, Stan Howard, Allan Howe, Lois Howell, Stephanie Inglezakis, Dorothy Jackson, Joey Lunn, Daniel Mainzer, David Mann, Russ Kinsey, Freddy Mohler, Jack Morran, Pat Nelman, Sue Nelman, Ray Rapoza, Ron Reed, Sandy Roser, Paula Schleis, Angie Seabeck, Fran Seabeck, Carol Slatter, Joe Stair, Ron Syroid, Pat Taylor, Brooks Townsend, Terry Townsend, Bob Troyer, Bob Turner, Whitey Wahl, and Bruce Winges.

Introduction

Myron Scott was 25 years old for most of the summer of 1933. That summer, as a photographer for the *Dayton Daily News*, Scott discovered a few boys racing their homemade cars down Big Hill Road. He snapped a few pictures and asked the boys to return and bring some friends.

A week later, Scott found nineteen boys waiting to race. One car in particular, the boxy "old number 7" built by Bob Gravett, caught Scott's eye. He snapped a photograph of it and it would become the Soap Box Derby's icon for 40 years. Scott had to be impressed by the turnout—if nineteen boys could show up in a week, how many entrants and fans could show up with added publicity?

The *Dayton Daily News* set August 19 as the race date, with heats starting at 1:30 PM. Entry blanks appeared in the newspaper and the race was open to all boys from Montgomery County, Ohio, under 16 years of age. Entry blanks would have to be received by August 14, and there was not an entry fee—the country was in the worst year of the Depression. Boys were encouraged to participate and could build their vehicles without worrying about weight or design limitations.

On race day, Scott had to be thrilled. The event attracted 362 soap boxers and a crowd of around 40,000 fans. Randy Custer was the fastest racer of the bunch. Scott realized that if the local race attracted this kind of following, a national event would not only be feasible, but successful.

Scott contacted a friend, Varley Young, a member of the creative division of the Campbell-Ewald Advertising Agency. General Motors was one of Campbell-Ewald's major accounts. Scott and Young decided to convince the firm that the support of a National Soap Box Derby would be "advertising well directed." The idea was floated to Chevrolet and the company's top brass liked what they heard and agreed to become the main sponsor of the race.

With capital in place, Scott contacted newspapers across the country to garner support for local races. This grassroots initiative would spread the Derby message to prospective participants in urban and rural areas. How could a young man resist the opportunity to "win fame, prizes, and a chance to star in the world's greatest Amateur racing event"?

Maybe it was happenstance or just sheer good luck, but Myron Scott saw the expanded potential of a local event and the All-American Soap Box Derby became a reality.

How I Saw It   1

THE 1930s
The Beginning

It all started with a news photographer who noticed boys racing down a hill in wooden vehicles. The man behind the camera was Myron Scott; the youths lived in Dayton, Ohio. Scott thought he could find more boys to race for the title of the fastest. The boys were having fun and the Soap Box Derby was born.

1933
News Sponsor Race: Open to All Boys Under 16 Years of Age, *Dayton Daily News* (OH)

1934
Soap Box Derby Sweeps Country, *Casa Grande Dispatch* (AZ)

1935
Saws Buzz, Hammers Pound as Juvenile Auto Racers Build Cars for '35 Derby, *Syracuse Herald* (NY)

1936
Boys, Attention. Another Thrilling Soap Box Derby to Be Held in El Paso, *El Paso Herald-Post* (TX)

1937
Come on Kids. You Can Sign Up Today and Get Your Rules Books for Soap Box Derby, *Helena Daily Independent* (MT)

1938
Lions Club Soap Box Derby Cars Will Be Checked and Placed on Display Friday Night, *Billings Gazette* (MT)

1939
Soap Box Derby Rules Simplified to Encourage All Young Boys to Enter, *Daily Mail* (MD)

Starting Down the Hill

When I was 22 years old, a buddy and I took a trip to Dayton, Ohio to interview Myron Scott for a book I planned on writing about the All-American Soap Box Derby. After all, I had been a part of the event since I could remember. My dad was involved with the race and I became fascinated with the summer spectacle, too.

Myron Scott, better known as Scottie, had previously worked for the *Dayton Daily News* and had snapped photos of boys piloting hand-made cars down Big Hill Road in June of 1933. Scott decided a larger race would generate reader interest and might provide some cheap enjoyment for economically-troubled Ohioans.

On August 19, 1933, 362 kids and a crowd of around 40,000 people showed up. The cars were a motley mix of all colors and sizes. Each driver had a "mechanic," who was allowed to give the racer a 15-foot shove at the start.

The boys-only event was won by Randy Custer. His machine was a blimpish looking, three-wheeled vehicle. Custer's car design might have been influenced by his father, Luzern, who was an associate of Orville Wright. Randy won a motor scooter, trophy, and a bouquet of flowers.

I guess the entry committee wasn't that diligent, since the second place finisher was a girl, Alice Johnson. Her prize was a boy's bike. It would be almost 40 years until girls were allowed in again.

1930s

A The relationship between the *Akron Beacon Journal* and the All-American Soap Box Derby started when the *Beacon Journal* sent its Soap Box winner to Dayton to compete in that year's race, 1934

B 362 kids competed in the local Dayton race on August 19. An estimated crowd of 40,000 watched them rumble down the hill, 1933

C The first article ever written about the Soap Box Derby in the *Dayton Daily News*, 1933

OPPOSITE PAGE Randy Custer, the champ for the first unofficial Soap Box Derby, receiving his awards, 1933

How I Saw It 5

Going National

Handicaps might make some horse races more competitive, but when it comes to Triple Crown races, all entrants carry the same weight. Maybe, Scottie (Myron E. Scott) and the first Derby board should have followed a similar path. Their decision propelled the wrong kid to the 1934 Soap Box Derby win.

When I went to see Scottie in 1975, I had a chance to ask about the Dayton event that brought local winners from 34 cities throughout the country to Burkhardt Hill. I always wondered how Jack Furstenberg lost. He had the fastest heat time, but ran a full ten seconds slower in the final. The winner was a boy from Muncie, IN, 11-year-old Robert Turner.

Scottie and the board had decided that handicapping the final would make for a better finish. Turner started down the hill 4.6 seconds before the other classification winner, Claude Alexander, and 5.7 seconds ahead of Furstenberg. Turner won by a mere 1.4 seconds. Scottie later admitted that he shouldn't have handicapped the cars. I told Scottie it was great that Turner won because he loved the Derby his entire life. After that first race, the Derby committee rescinded the handicap rule much to the joy of thousands of entrants from 1934 on.

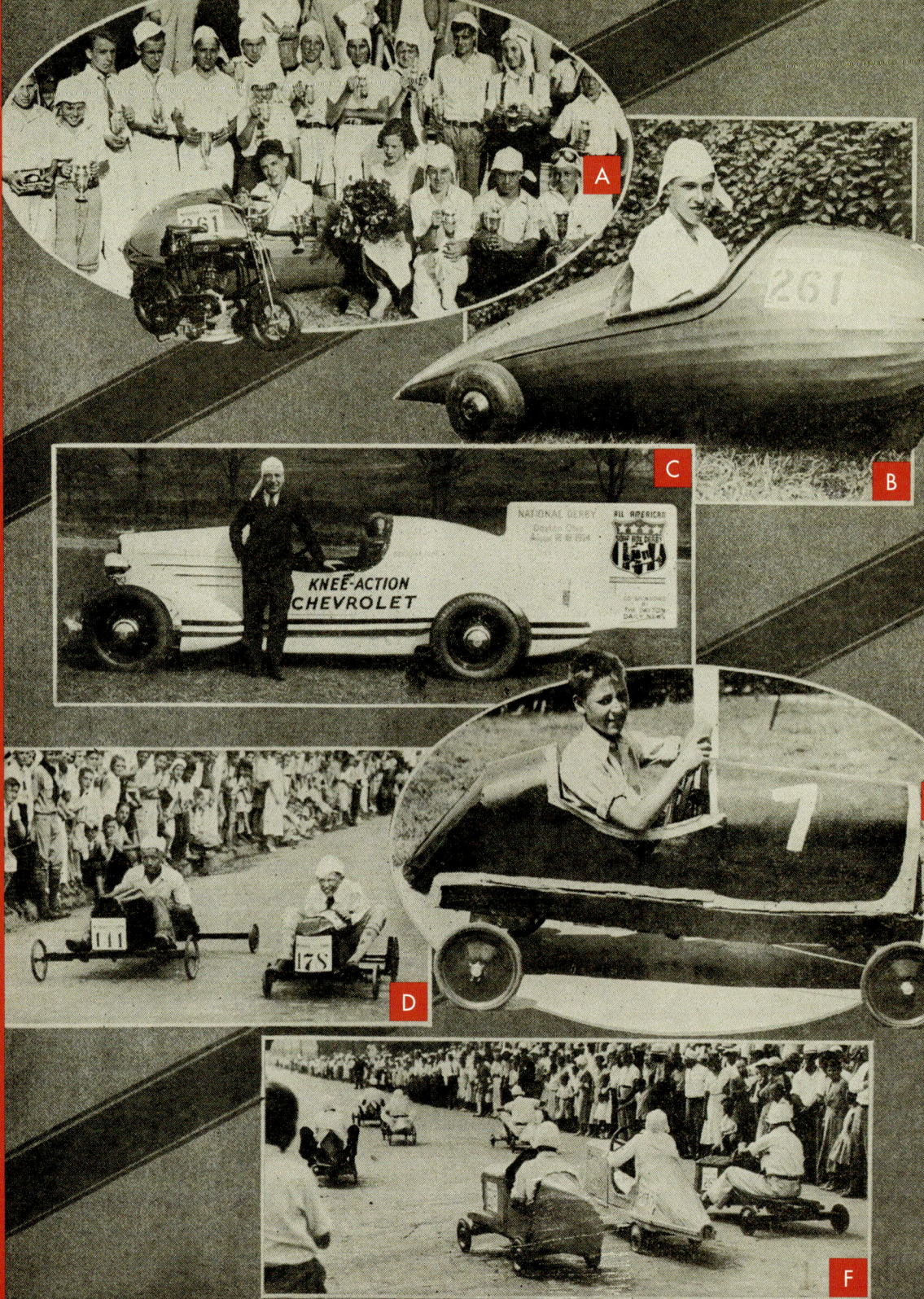

1930s

A The champions' cars, including Paul Brown's car from Oklahoma City, being fixed in the pits, 1936

B Derby helmet factory in Detroit, MI. White helmets were used in the local races from 1937–1939, 1937

C Derby General Manager, Jack Gormley, and his assistant, Harry Hartz, with the Derby promotional car they took to the New York World's Fair, 1937

OPPOSITE PAGE

A A group of the winners, with Alice Johnson, the only girl driver that day, 1933

B Randall Custer, winner, who led the field in his three wheel special, 1933

C Myron E. Scott, and the Chevrolet 'special', which made a 7,000 mile tour contacting various newspapers, 1933

D A close finish, 1933

E Bob Gravett, Oakwood, OH, who was one of the first entries in the first Soap Box race. Gravett drove No. 7 in the Blue Flame race, 1933

F A general view of a 'heat' start, 1933

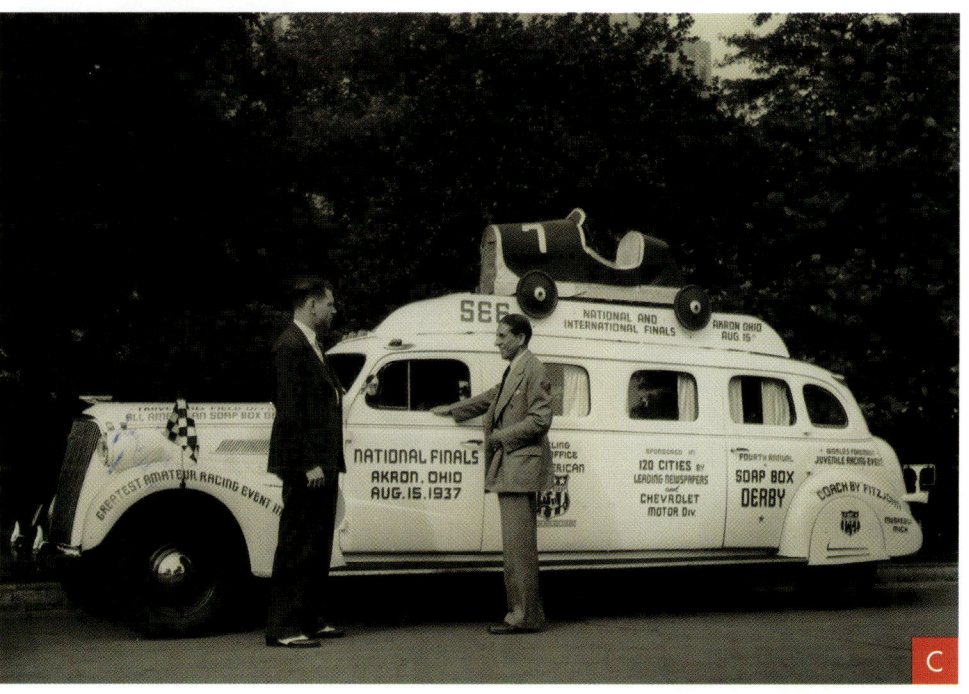

How I Saw It   7

A In the early years, kids were allowed to sled down the hill at Derby Downs, 1937

B Left to right: Jim Schlimmer, *Akron Beacon Journal*; Myron Scott, Derby founder; Shorty Fulton, airport and track director; Ed Hedner and Varley Young, Campbell-Ewald Agency; and an unidentified man at Derby Downs during its construction, 1936

C Aerial view of Derby Downs in Akron, OH, 1936

How I Saw It

1930s

A Robert Turner from Muncie, IN, won 1st place in the first National Soap Box Championship, 1934

B "Old No. 7" built by Robert Gravett, son of a Dayton metal stamping plant employee, competed in the first race. Although it didn't win, Myron Scott chose it as the symbol of the Derby for the next 40 years, 1933

C First heat of the All-American Soap Box Derby at Derby Downs, 1936

How I Saw It   9

STARTING GRID

Professional Drivers At the Derby

Bill Cummings   1934–1935

Wilbur Shaw   1937–1954

Maurie Rose   1953

Bob Sweikert   1955

Bobby Unser   1971

Bobby Allison   1976, 2000

Dale Earnhardt   1988

Dick Simon   1988

John Andretti   1991

Lyn St. James   1992, 2004

Tom Sneva   1993

Jerry Nadeau   2002

Ricky Craven   2002–2004

Joe Nemecheck   2003–2004

Tony Stewart   2003–2004

Erin Crocker   2005

Jimmy Johnson   2006

10   How I Saw It

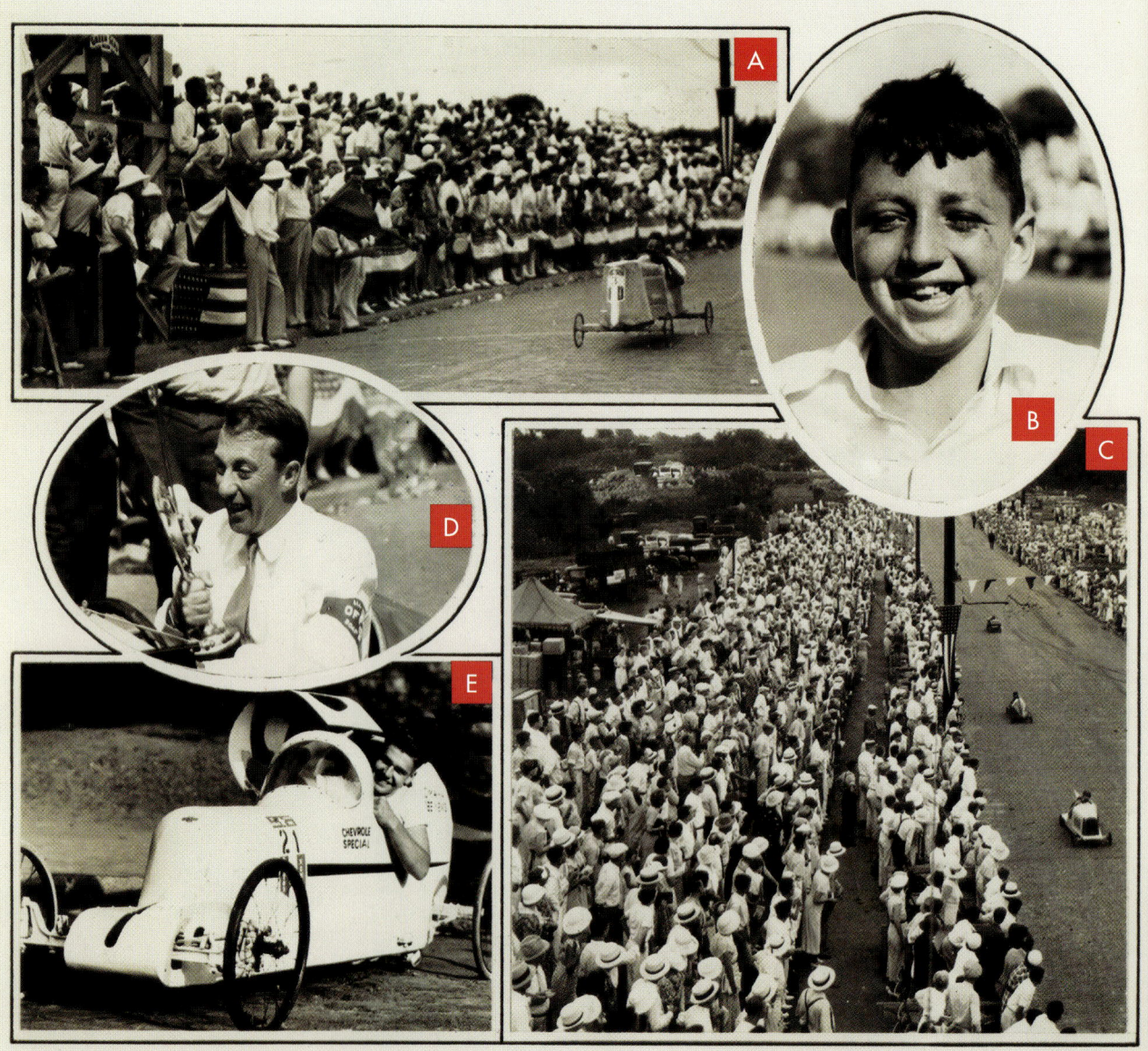

1934
Muncie Youth Wins National Soap Box Championship

Eleven-year-old Robert Turner (photo No. 2) of Muncie, Ind., won the national championship, four years in college, and the plaudits of 60,000 watchers, as he flashed (photo No. 1) across the finish line at Dayton, Ohio, in the first annual All-American Soap Box Derby, sponsored by 34 leading American newspapers and the Chevrolet Motor Company. Part of the huge crowd is pictured in No. 3. Graham McNamee, famous NBC sports announcer, who described the Derby on a nationwide radio hook-up, is shown (No. 4) as he broadcast while traveling down the graded course in a typical soap box racer. Jack Furstenberg, 15, of Omaha, won the E. V. Rickenbacker trophy for the fastest heat, and the Charles F. Kettering cup for the best constructed racer (No. 5). This was the only "closed job" entered in this year's event, in which 34 champions from as many cities were selected by time trials from more than 20,000 boys who built and raced their own creations.

1930s

A A race in Australia with unusual cars, including a toothpaste car in the far lane, 1939

B The starting line at the Elizabeth Port, South Africa race where there were reported to be 80,000 spectators on hand, 1935

OPPOSITE PAGE

A Robert Turner crosses the finish line at Dayton, Ohio, in the first annual All-American Soap Box Derby, 1934

B Eleven-year-old Robert Turner of Muncie, IN, national champion, 1934

C Part of the huge crowd, 1934

D Graham McNamee broadcasts nationwide while traveling down the course in a soap box racer, 1934

E Jack Furstenberg, of Omaha, NE, won the E. V. Rickenbacker trophy for the fastest heat, and the Charles F. Kettering cup for the best constructed racer, 1934

How I Saw It   11

MY SOAP BOX

The Crash that Brought Fame

In 1985, Paul Brown came back to Akron with his grandson. This Paul Brown, however, wasn't the famous football coach and innovator—this Paul Brown drove in the 1935 Derby, and by accident garnered immense publicity for the event.

Graham McNamee, the sports voice of America, and local NBC baseball broadcaster, Tom Manning, were on hand in 1935 to report the Soap Box Derby action to a huge radio audience. Rumor had it the two had had some lunch at a local bar, and their senses might have suffered a bit. In one of the afternoon heats, Paul Brown came tearing down the track in his car and slammed into the men. The call went out for aid, and Billow's funeral home's ambulance service responded. McNamee and Manning were taken to the hospital.

As the saying goes, any publicity is good publicity. The accident provided more advertising than the Derby could ever have afforded. Newspapers and radio stations, nationwide, covered the story. *Time* magazine (8/19/1935) wrote about McNamee and the crash. The question of "What the hey is the Soap Box Derby" got answered.

McNamee ended up leaving for his summer home with minor injuries. Manning suffered a cracked vertebra, and I was told he walked with a limp the rest of his life. Maurice Bale weathered the squelching temperatures, had good wheels, and came in first.

A The final heat of the first annual race at Derby Downs in Akron, OH, when Mauri Bale from Anderson, IN, came in 1st, Everett Miller from St. Louis, MO, came in 2nd, and Loney Kline from Akron, OH, came in 3rd, 1935

B A wreck at the Akron local. No one was seriously injured, 1939

C All-American banquet at the Mayflower Hotel in Akron, 1935

D Paul Brown of Oklahoma City, 1935

OPPOSITE PAGE Graham McNamee smiling from the ambulance where he received treatment for injuries sustained when the car driven by Paul Brown drove into him, 1935

1930s

How I Saw It   13

MY SOAP BOX

Poor Dickie Ballard

Over my years at the Derby, several people have come to the track and indicated they had won the Derby. Few really have. During the festivities in 1981, one guy came in and said his picture was still on the wall. I looked him over and knew the returnee was Bob Ballard, the 1937 world champion.

Ballard of White Plains, New York used his scholarship to pursue a career in engineering. Prior to that he was also a Navy man. Bob was a unique guy, covering 14,200 miles of the country, visiting parks and old Navy buddies before attending college. He was still convinced his brother, Dickie, had been robbed of the 1938 Derby.

Richard "Dickie" Ballard raced down the hill neck and neck with Bobby Berger. At first, Derby staffers thought Dickie had won. They brought him and his car back to the finish line where a throng of reporters waited to interview the new world champ. Word got out that Bobby Berger of Nebraska had actually won in a photo finish. Reporters abandoned the poor boy and he began to sob, tears welling up in his eyes. Finally, a Derby official told him that coming in second won him a new Chevy. Dickie perked up immediately.

I showed a photograph of the finish line to Bob Ballard. I told him to look at his expression. It wasn't one of glee. "You know," he said, "I think you finally got me convinced."

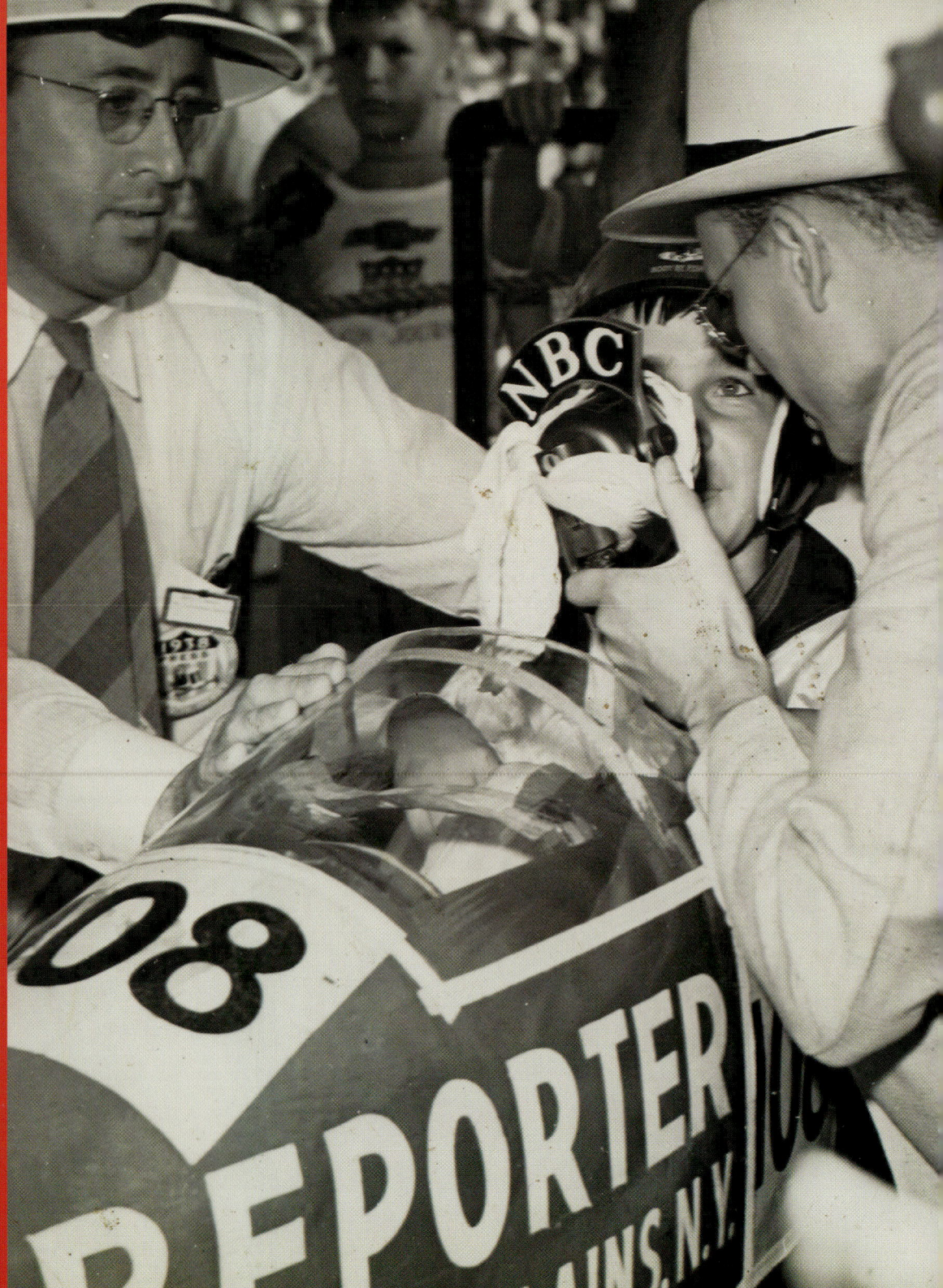

A World Champion Bob Berger raced shirtless to victory over Dick Ballard. Pictured here left to right with J. H. Keating, Chevrolet Sales Manager; Wilbur Shaw; and Jack Gormley, General Manager of the Derby, 1938

B World Champion Bob Ballard from White Plains, NY, with his trophies, 1937

OPPOSITE PAGE Dick Ballard from White Plains, NY, was initially thought to be the winner. Dick Ballard being interviewed by the press before the real winner was announced, 1938

1930s

How I Saw It

THE 1940s
A Great Start

In the early 1940s, the Derby was beginning to expand. Local Derby champions were feted grandly when they arrived in Akron for the national finals. WWII put a hold on Derby action for several years, but with renewed energy, Chevrolet and local newspapers relaunched the national event in 1946. The cars were speeding downhill once again.

1940
Boys Busy Building Coasters for Soap Box Derby to Be Held on Ralston Hill Next Thursday, *Reno Evening Gazette* (NV)

1941
Speed, Not Beauty: That's What to Seek in Soap Box Racer, *Burlington Daily Times-News* (NC)

1942
Soap Box Derby Will Be Staged Here October 12, *Lowell Sun* (MA)

1943
Legion Soap Box Derby on July 5, *Daily Courier* (PA)

1944
Derby Races to Highlight 5-Day Frolic, *Vidette Messenger* (IN)

1945
Soap Box Derby Brought Out Large Crowd, *Monticello* (IA)

1946
Derby Downs Is Ready for Big National Race Day, *Daily-Times-News* (VT)

1947
WTIP to Air Finals of Soap Box Derby, *Charleston Gazette* (WV)

1948
Saturday Show for Area Boys Will Launch Derby Drive Here, *Lubbock Avalanche-Journal* (TX)

1949
Soap Box Derby Champion on Radio, *Janesville Daily Gazette* (WI)

A Officials wore striped shirts so they were easy to spot at a distance. Here are four officials from left to right: Bruce Overbey, Myron Scott, Shorty Fulton, and Jim Schlemmer, with Jimmy Stewart in the middle, 1948

B Three-time Indy Champion Wilbur Shaw (left), and World Champion Tommy Fisher, 1940

C Cleveland's Derby champ, Bill Zoller (middle), showing his trophy to Ty Cobb, Babe Ruth, and Tris Speaker at Cleveland Municipal Stadium, 1941

D One of the first live TV broadcasts of the Derby in Akron, 1949

E The three founders and first three inductees in the All-American Soap Box Derby Hall of Fame from left to right—Jim Schlemmer, Myron Scott, and B. E. "Shorty" Fulton, 1946

How I Saw It

A The All-American Awards Show at the Akron Armory. The top 6 boys won trophies and prizes, 1940

B Pre-race parade with the first nine World Champions leading the way, 1947

C Camp Y-Noah, located just south of Akron, became a place where the champs could relax and have fun before the race opened, 1948

D Race day at Derby Downs, 1941

E The first six of seven World Champions from left to right—Bob Turner, Mauri Bale, Herb Muench, Tom Fisher, Cliff Hardesty, and Bob Ballard. Missing: Bob Berger, 1941

1940s

How I Saw It

Fastest Heats

In 1934, Jack Furstenberg went 1,980 ft. in 51.06 secs. on the Dayton track

In 1935, Loney Kline went 1181 ft. in 30.40 secs. on the Tallmadge Hill track

In 1939, Cliff Hardesty went 1175 ft. in 27.80 secs. on the Derby Downs track

In 1940, Tom Fisher went 1000 ft. in 26.30 secs. on the Derby Downs track

In 1947, Tony Penuelas went 975.4 ft. in 26.63 secs. on the Derby Downs track

In 1974, Ed Myers went 953.75 ft. in 27.10 secs. on the Derby Downs track

In 2004, Hilary Pearson went 989.4 ft. in 28.24 secs. on the Derby Downs track

CHEVROLET MOTOR DIVISION
GENERAL MOTORS SALES CORPORATION
DETROIT, MICHIGAN
GENERAL MOTORS BUILDING

December 11, 1941.

Mr. John S. Knight
Publisher
Akron Beacon-Journal
Akron, Ohio

Dear Mr. Knight:

    Because of conditions now prevailing, it has been decided to suspend the Soap Box Derby for 1942. We will review the matter again in the fall of 1942 and, if conditions at that time warrant, we will, with your co-operation, resume this great boys' activity.

    We regret, like everyone else, the necessity for this decision but we are sure that the reasons are perfectly obvious to you - first, the emergency at hand will require the energies of everyone of us to bring it to a successful conclusion; second, the inability of the wheel manufacturers to secure the needed materials to complete the wheel sets, these metals being required elsewhere; third, the need for conserving the rubber supply.

    It is our sincere hope that we can count on your wholehearted assistance and support with the resumption of the program at a later date, because of its fine contribution to the youth of America.

    Again we want to say that we have appreciated your fine, loyal co-operation and the cordial relations we have experienced in the development of this activity. It has been a real pleasure to work with you.

Sincerely yours,

C. P. Fisken
W

Manager, Advertising Division

1940s

A The picture was a promotional shot for the Derby with George Burns and Gracie Allen. They visited Akron to promote the race, but not on Derby day, 1946

B Akron won the national race for the third time in 1949, when Freddy Derks (top) of Akron, OH, crossed the finish line ahead of Charles Muhl of Cleveland, OH, and Don Klepsch of Detroit, MI, 1949

C Starting line at Derby Downs. The current Akron track, a Works Progress Administration project, is the oldest official Soap Box Derby course in the country. At present, it measures 989.4 foot in length, but that distance has changed many times over the years. Each lane is 10 foot wide. The hill has an eleven-degree slope that tapers down to one percent at the bottom, 1941

OPPOSITE PAGE Letter from Chevrolet about the suspension of the Derby due to WWII, 1941

How I Saw It 21

All Hail Akron

Claude Smith holds the title as the longest reigning Derby champion. He happened to win the race in the summer of 1941. The Day of Infamy and subsequent global events halted the Derby from 1942 through 1945.

The number "1" became a special number for Claude and all of Akron. In 1941, piloting Car 1, in Lane 1, the 1-4 (14)-year-old Claude drove his shiny black speedster to victory in the All-American Soap Box Derby and became Number 1 in the world of gravity car racing. Finally, a home-grown Akronite had taken the title. Claude said the car cost $10 and 10 months of hard work.

I met Claude in 1966, and we have been friends since. He came to my wedding—before that I dated his sister-in-law, Jackie. Claude and his brother, George, who placed third in the 1940 Derby, donated their trophies to the Derby Museum. Claude attended Hiram College before earning a college degree from Kent State University. He ended up building two houses and attributed much of his construction ability to assembling his Derby car.

Claude raced again in the Derby as part of the 2009 Oil Can Race, along with the 89-year-old Mike Politz and the 91-year-old John Fraser. Politz won the race, but Smith got the last laugh. He said his biggest thrill, since he was only 82 years old, was "being called 'the kid.'"

A World Champion Tom Fisher holds the all-time track record, 26.30 seconds in the All-American Soap Box Derby, 1940

B Semi-final heat when Harold Hayes from Durham, NC, placed 4th to become the first African American to place, 1946

C Local champions with the Alaska champion, Leo Osterman, 1946

D World Champion Fred Derks of Akron, OH, with his mother and Wilbur Shaw, 1949

1940s

OPPOSITE PAGE World Champion Claude Smith from Akron, OH, with Wilbur Shaw and Claude's mother, 1941

How I Saw It 23

MY SOAP BOX

The Graphite Kid

Derby cars reach speeds up to 50 mph. Crashes have ruined cars and caused injuries. Of course, these mishaps usually occur during actual heats. Gil Klecan's smash-up was the exception.

In 1983, a guy walked into the Derby offices out of the blue and growled, "Hi, I won the Derby, but I got the graphite off now." Standing in front of me was the Boy Scout from San Diego, California who became known as the "Graphite Kid." In order to cut down on wind resistance in the 1946 Derby, he smeared himself and his car with graphite. Gil glided to victory with the crowd backing him.

The story could have ended for Klecan at that point. However, a Warner Brothers film crew wanted some newsreel footage. They set up a camera on the back of a station wagon and asked Klecan to follow the vehicle down the Derby hill. The crew and Klecan descended. Suddenly, the station wagon's driver heard a shout of "stop!" The car stopped, but Klecan kept right on going and crashed into the station wagon. The idea was to stop filming.

Klecan continued to the hospital with scrapes, bruises, head trauma, and two fractured vertebrae. I was told that Chevrolet donated $5,000 to help Klecan get better. Klecan recovered and was smart enough to use the windfall to start his successful real estate business.

24

1940s

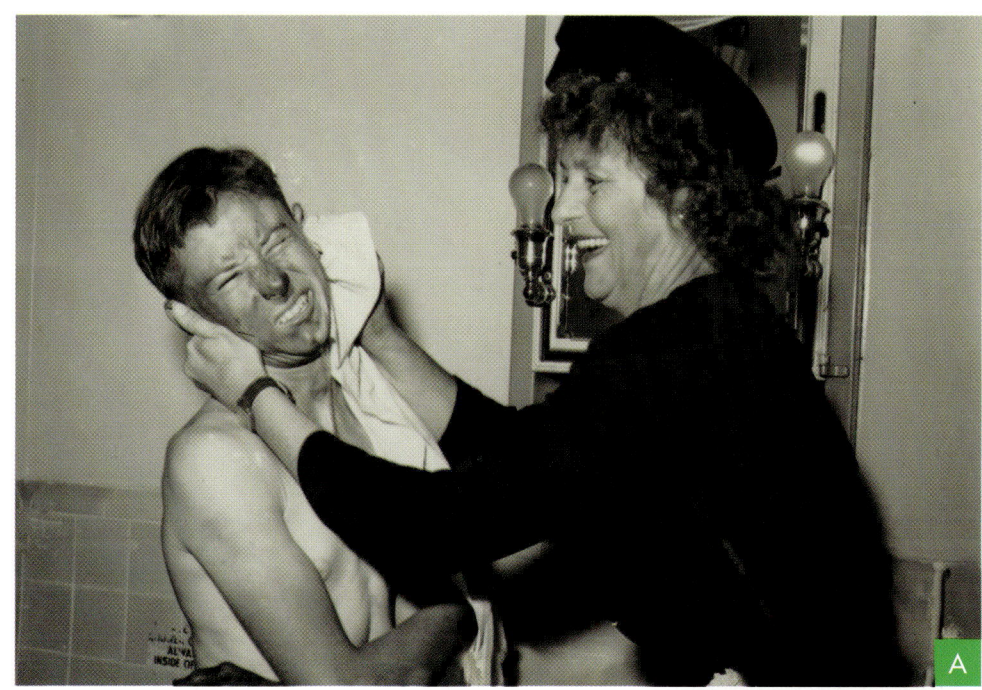

A & B Gilbert Klecan's mother trying to wash the graphite off of the World Champion's face, 1946

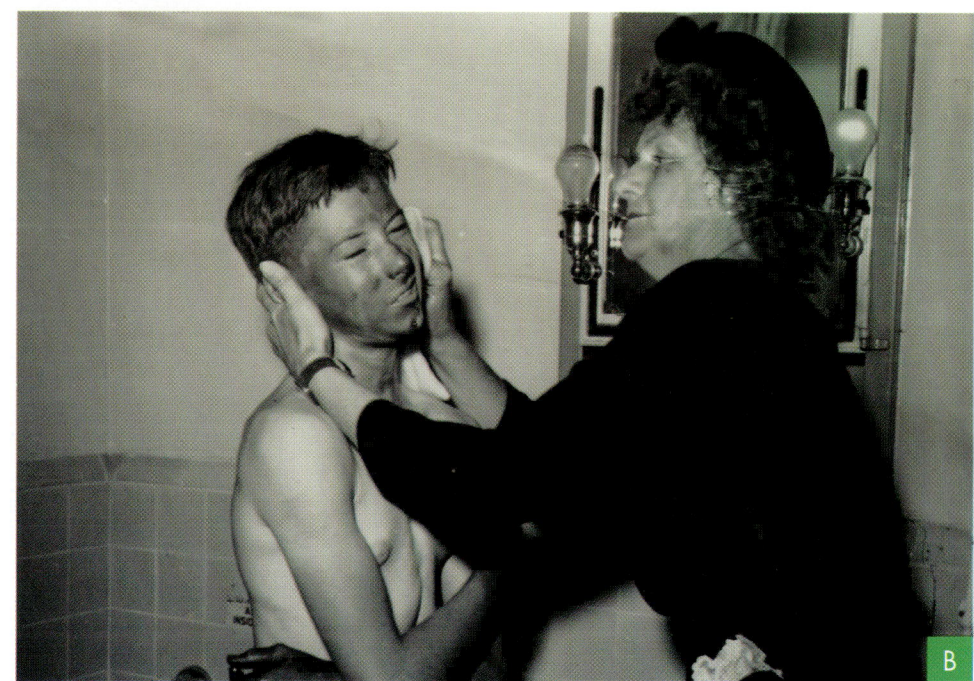

OPPOSITE PAGE Gil Klecan from San Diego, CA, "The Graphite Kid," shown here with his mother and father, receiving his trophy. He got the nickname after he smeared himself and his car with graphite, hoping it would help him glide down the hill faster, 1946

How I Saw It 25

THE 1950s
Seasoned Champions

The Derby was becoming the event for young boys in the United States. Word was spreading overseas, too. Celebrities were beginning to show up for the national finals, adding even more publicity to the event. Derby winners were held in high esteem. America was growing and the Derby was a barometer of the continued prosperity.

1950
German Champion Enters 1950 National Derby Race, Mansfield News-Journal (OH)

1951
Parents and Sons Invited to Soap Box Derby Program, Chronicle-Express (NY)

1952
Annual Soap Box Derby Race Held in Darlington in June, Florence Morning News (SC)

1953
Derby Champion Gets Set for "Dream Trip" to Akron, Bismarck Tribune (ND)

1954
Last Year's Derby Winner Worked Two Years on His Car, Daily Capital News (MO)

1955
Powell Boy 11, Wins Bozeman Soap Box Derby, Billings Gazette (MT)

1956
61 Boys Register for City Box Derby; Winner to Race in National Event in Ohio, Fairbanks Daily News-Miner

1957
Lehi Boy, Family Back from Soap Box Derby in Akron, Daily Herald (UT)

1958
1958 Soap Box Derby Begins at Johnson AB, Pacific Stars and Stripes

1959
Nixon to Watch Soap Box Derby, Leader-Times (PA)

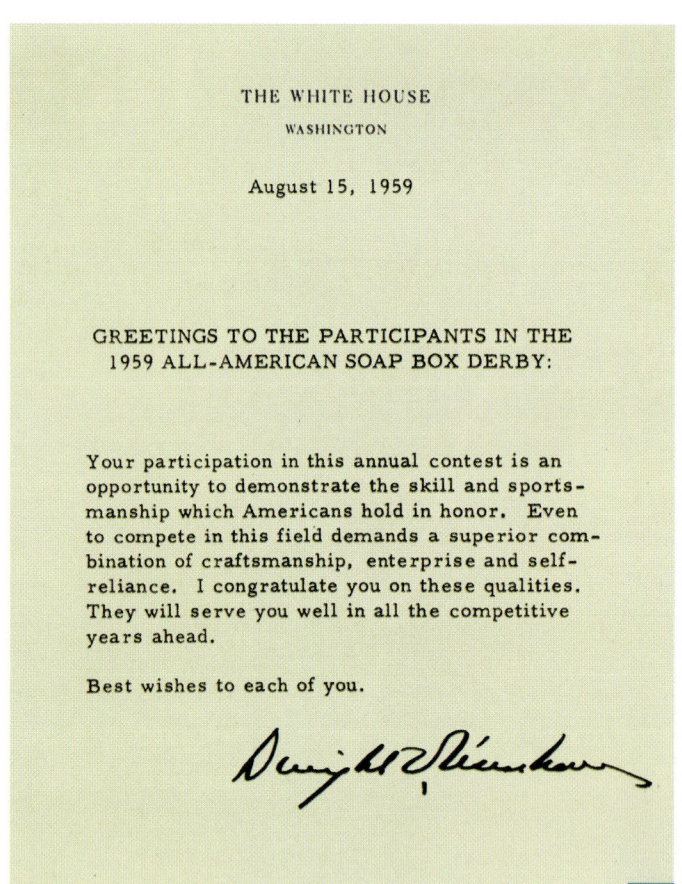

A Parade of Champions, 1955

B Vic Shepherd (left) from Flint, MI, Jim Thomas from Williamsport, PA, and Joey Lunn (right) from Columbus, GA, at the finish line of the final heat. Thomas had a chance to beat Lunn in the national race but he sat upright too soon. When he was later asked why he didn't keep his head down, Thomas said that he thought he had already crossed the finish line, 1952

C This letter from President Eisenhower was printed in the program, 1959

D When the Soap Box Derby first began, kids used just about any kind of wheels they could find, including those from old bicycles and baby buggies. Goodrich and Firestone manufactured the first sanctioned wheels in 1937, in plants like this, 1952

28   How I Saw It

A Danny Doupe from Rochester, NY, and Brian Hancock (front) from Mission City, B.C., Canada just after their crash in the first heat. The crew was able to fix Hancock's car so he could continue racing. He won the U.S. guest trophy, 1959

B World Champion Terry Townsend of Anderson, IN, with his parents and younger brother (top), Barney, who would go on to win in 1959, 1957

1950s

How I Saw It   29

A Slick Ride

The Kentucky Derby has its blanket of roses. The Indianapolis 500 has its jug of milk. The All-American Soap Box Derby has its Oil Can Trophy.

In the early summer of 1950, Wilbur Shaw, the three-time Indianapolis 500 winner, challenged anyone to race him in a Soap Box Derby type car. Jimmy Stewart and Jack Dempsey said "why not." Dempsey's six-wheeled vehicle beat Stewart's "jet job" entry. Stewart's car had tubes on it to let air pass through, decreasing resistance. Shaw's "secret weapon" had a vertical stack of pipes on the rear of the car for extra speed. At the banquet following the Derby, Shaw ribbed Dempsey for stealing 400 pounds of lead from Shaw's car. Shaw said he would have won otherwise.

The next year a small-time actor, Ronald Reagan, who would go on to become the President of the United States, joined the festivities. He raced against actor Andy Devine and the ventriloquist Paul Winchell. Winchell piloted his car along with his dummy, who, unknown to the crowd, was only lending mental support. Obviously, the legless dummy provided some great advice, as Winchell won easily. Reagan finished second and Devine a distant third. The crowd got its biggest thrill after the finish when about six mechanics had to use a crowbar and saw to extract the rotund Devine from his racer.

A According to Derby records the first official celebrity "Oil Can Race" was held at the start of the decade. Jack Dempsey won the race. Here, Dempsey (center) accepts the trophy from a Chevrolet executive, W. E. Fish, with Jimmy Stewart, William Boyd, and Wilbur Shaw, 1950

B Left to right in rear: Roy Rogers, George Montgomery, and Jimmy Stewart. Left to right in front: Dale Evans and Dinah Shore. At the twentieth anniversary race, they were on hand to cheer the racers from the champions' stand, 1957

C Left to right: Celebrities Guy Madison, Pat Boone, and Eddie Bracken cheered the champ from the stands, 1958

D Left to right: Jimmy Stewart, Edgar Bergen, World Champion Joey Lunn, and Joe E. Brown with Lunn's damaged car, 1952

1950s

OPPOSITE PAGE Comedy team, Bud Abbott (right) and Lou Costello, clowning around in their Derby shirts, 1954

How I Saw It   31

STARTING GRID

Famous Celebrities At the Derby

Abbott & Costello
1954

Lorne Greene
1962, 1964, 1969, 1970, 1971

Tom Hanks
1981

Rock Hudson
1963

Elizabeth Montgomery
1966

Richard Nixon
1959

Ronald Reagan
1951

Roy Rogers
1956, 1957

Dinah Shore
1953, 1955, 1957

James Stewart
1947–1950, 1952, 1957

A Bud Abbott flagging Jack Carson (top car), Bob Cummings, and Lou Costello, 1954

B Andy Devine with his many fans, 1951

32   *How I Saw It*

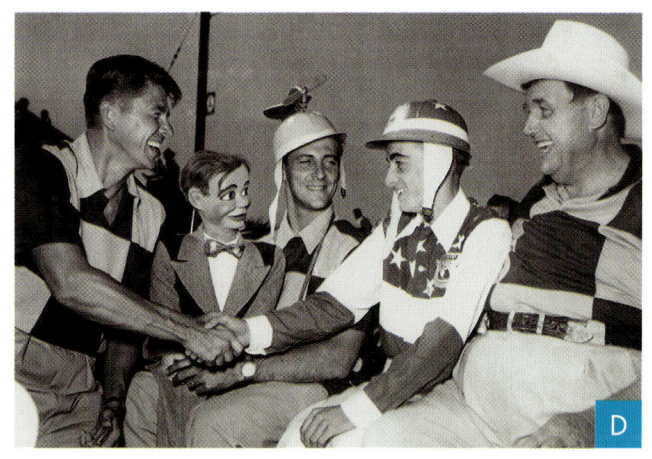

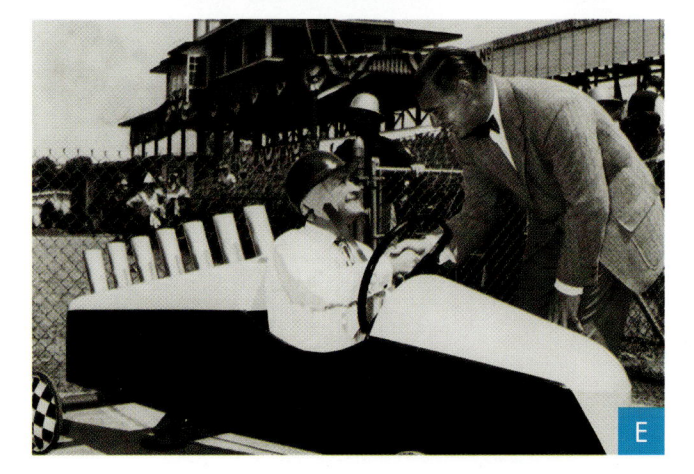

A Vice-President Richard Nixon flagging the first heat. Two of the three cars crashed on their way down the hill, 1959

B Champion Barney Townsend of Anderson, IN; his mother; his older brother, Terry (top left), an All-American Champion; and Richard Nixon (middle), 1957

C Jack Carson (center) was presented with the Oil Can Trophy by Will Power, President of Chevrolet, with Bud Abbott and Lou Costello (left), and Bob Cummings (right), 1954

D Ronald Reagan shaking hands with the winner, Darwin Cooper, with Paul Winchell and Andy Devine (right) watching on, 1951

E Wilbur Shaw, three-time Indianapolis Race winner and frequent visitor to the All-American, showing off his car to Clark Gable. Shaw would race in the Oil Can at Derby Downs later that year, 1950

How I Saw It   33

MY SOAP BOX

Loopholes and Holey Wheels

Stretching the rules became a contest within the contest, beginning in the 1950s. Fame propels even young competitors to find ways to propel their cars as fast as possible. As media outlets grew, the winner of the All-American became a celebrity.

My good friend, "Steady Freddy" Mohler, who won the Derby in 1953, rolled down the hill on wheels that were drilled out and looked like Swiss cheese. Joey Lunn, the 11-year-old from Georgia, didn't do anything illegal in winning the 1952 event, but Derby workers who slipped on three new and very fast wheels after Lunn's crash helped him cross the finish line as a winner. Dick Rohrer, who won the All-American in 1955, was rumored to have soaked his wheels in gasoline for added speed. Terry Townsend's wheels barely passed the circumference test, but when they did, Woodroe, Terry's dad, exclaimed, "The race is over." Terry went onto win the 1957 Derby with ease.

I was able to roll with some of these guys later in my life. Joey Lunn was the best man at my wedding and Terry Townsend was a groomsman—I had a great advantage, too.

A Terry Townsend from Anderson, IN, won the championship and a trip to Europe for two weeks. His mother, Honey, painted the stars on his car, 1957

B World Champion Dick Kemp, from Los Angeles, CA, with his parents. He is the brother of Jack Kemp who was a NFL football player and politician, 1954

C Jimmy Dean, accepting the Oil Can Trophy from William Power, President of Chevrolet. Dean is flanked by Art Carney (left) and Wendell Corey (behind Power), 1950

D Champion Kenneth Johnson and his family from Roanoke, VA, who arrived by a specially decorated Eastern Air Lines plane, were met by one of the official Soap Box Derby cars and a motorcycle escort, 1952

1950s

OPPOSITE PAGE Freddy Mohler of Muncie, IN, the winner, with Bob Turner on the left and his mother and father on the right, 1953

How I Saw It 35

STARTING GRID

Other Nations At the Derby

Australia

Canada

Germany

Guam

Ireland

Japan

Mexico

New Zealand

Panama

Philippines

Puerto Rico

South Africa

Venezuela

A The All-American Soap Box Derby staff has consisted of approximately twelve full-time employees and more than 700 volunteers. More than 8,000 Derby volunteers help out each year throughout the country, 1955

B Derby Downs on race day. Chevrolet was the Derby's main sponsor from 1936 through 1972, 1957

36   How I Saw It

A World Champion Jim Miley, who at 6'1" was the tallest Derby champion, standing by his "cigar car," 1958

B At the end of this race the wrong winner was announced, which meant Peter Christlief from Los Angeles, CA, was able to go on to the finals even though he didn't win his heat. He placed 5th—winning a trophy and a $1,000 scholarship, 1958

C Akron officials with Chevrolet's Derby General Manager, Jake King, planning the 19th race, 1956

D The Welcome Ceremonies at the Mayflower Hotel. Every champ from 1935–1969 was welcomed there. The Garfield High Band was the official band, 1952

1950s

How I Saw It   37

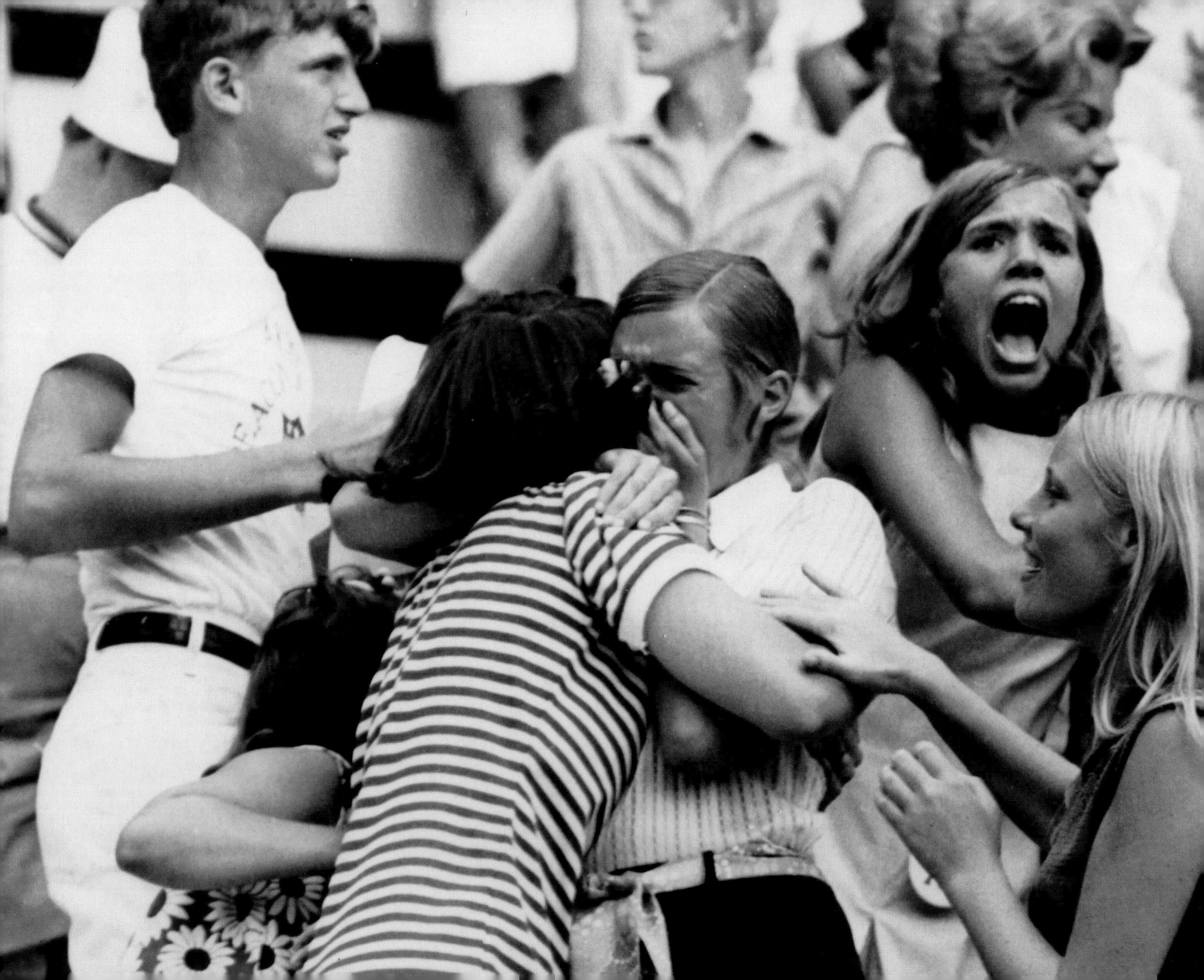

THE 1960s
Hey Days

The Derby was still going strong in the early part of the 1960s. The U.S. would outdo the Soviets and land a man on the moon by the end of the decade. Television was blossoming. Still, unrest was beginning to paint the American landscape. The "generation gap" was widening and the American way of life was changing, but local Derby champions still kept coming to Akron.

1960
Spang Kids Get Bid to Soap Box Derby, *European Stars and Stripes*

1961
Boy Who Heeded Dad Wins Soap Box Derby, *Newport Daily News* (RI)

1962
Petersburg Lad Wins 2 Heats, Then Loses, *Progress-Index* (VA)

1963
Soap Box Derby Queen Is Selected, *Oshkosh Daily Northwestern* (WI)

1964
3,000 Expected for Derby Day, *Oneonta Star* (NY)

1965
Derby Clinic Slated Saturday for Drivers, *News-Palladium* (MI)

1966
Derby Days in Full Swing at Clearfield, *Progress* (PA)

1967
244 Compete for National Soap Box Derby in Akron, *Weirton Daily Times* (WV)

1968
Local Soap Box Derby One of 26 New Derbys, *Daily Journal* (MN)

1969
Soap Box Derby Creates a Furor, *Salina Journal* (KS)

A Herb Alpert, musician and co-founder of A&M Records, getting ready for the Oil Can race, 1968

B Pernell Roberts (top), Michael Landon, and Dan Blocker (bottom) competing in the Oil Can race, 1964

C World Champion Kenny Cline in his "grasshopper car," with Chevrolet's president, Pete Estes, 1967

D David Mann of Gary, IN, celebrates winning the silver anniversary race, 1962

E The trophies that went to the top 9 winners of the 29th All-American, 1966

40   How I Saw It

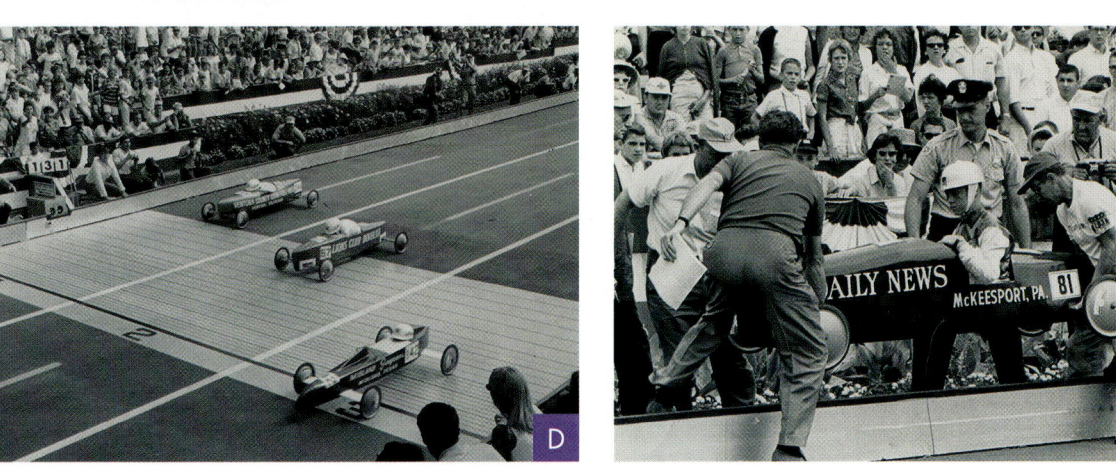

A Cars having weight checked on the official weigh station, 1962

B Jim Simpson from Greenville, SC, and Bill Peters (right) from Missoula, MT, ran off the track in a first round wreck, 1965

C Okinawa's Teruo Hanashiro; first time down the hill his racer flipped and crashed, spilling him on the track, 1967

D Final heat where Steve Souter from Midland, TX, beat Dick Behan from Dover, NH, and Dave Quinn from Ventura, CA, for the first lay-down car victory, 1969

E Terry Lesko from McKeesport, PA, crashed his car in the semi-final heat. He managed to win 9th place even though his car was damaged beyond repair, 1961

How I Saw It   41

MY SOAP BOX

My Trip to Derby Downs

When running contests, like raffling off a trip to Tahiti, sponsors prohibit their employees from entering. People tend to think families of sponsors might have gotten their names drawn in a less than random fashion. Winning becomes suspicious.

As I grew up around the Derby, I always had the dream of racing in the event. I witnessed the joy of victorious drivers and the accolades they received, not to mention the prizes and trips. The winners became instant heroes and big celebrities when they went back home.

In 1937, Shorty Fulton's son Bud was in the Derby and for the second year in a row, finished second. My father heard that Bud was booed. After all, Shorty had helped build Derby Downs and was in charge of the track. Bud got help, right?

For that reason, my father wouldn't allow me to qualify for the Derby. Maybe the crowd reaction would have been too much for him. I did, however, have the good fortune of racing in 1966, due to an airline strike. The Okinawa champ couldn't get to Akron, and I was selected as a substitute for the race and given all the perks that go along with participating. The thrill of speeding down the Derby hill is something I remember vividly to this day. Unlike my father, I've let my two girls race. No one booed them.

Jeff Iula

THE WHITE HOUSE
WASHINGTON

Congratulations to each of you for having gained the finals of the 1962 All-American Soap Box Derby.

The craftsmanship and sportsmanship you have displayed in attaining the high level of competition are most commendable. Your achievements are an inspiration to all the youth of America.

My best wishes to you in the finals.

John F. Kennedy

A

A This letter from President Kennedy was printed in the program, 1962

B Robert Russell Bennett, who wrote the official Derby March, directed all nine Akron school bands in the inaugural performance, 1966

C Substitute driver Jeff Iula in the Okinawa champ's car during his first heat, 1966

D This letter from President Johnson was printed in the program, 1965

1960s

THE WHITE HOUSE
WASHINGTON
July 1, 1965

TO THE FINALISTS IN THE 1965
ALL-AMERICAN SOAP BOX DERBY:

I am pleased to extend my personal greetings and congratulations to each of you. This event has become a traditional test of the mettle and mechanical skill of American youth, and you have demonstrated these qualities in abundance. I am confident that your performance here will strengthen our faith in our native ingenuity and know-how.

Good luck and best wishes.

Lyndon B. Johnson

OPPOSITE PAGE Jeff Iula, substituting for Raymond Rapoza, the champ from Okinawa, riding down the track in a 1965 Corvette convertible, 1966

How I Saw It 43

STARTING GRID

The Derby on the Little Screen

Make Room for Daddy, Season 5, Episode 11, "The Soap Box Derby." Original Air Date, December 16, 1957

My Three Sons, Season 1, Episode 27, "Soap Box Derby." Original Air Date, March 30, 1961

Bewitched, Season 3, Episode 16, "Soapbox Derby." Original Air Date, December 29, 1966

Dennis the Menace, Season 2, Episode 30, "The Soapbox Derby." Original Air Date, April 30, 1961

The Waltons, Season 8, Episode 20, "The Last Straw." Original Air Date, February 7, 1980

The Care Bears Family, Season 1, Episode 3, "Lucky Charm/Soap Box Derby." Original Air Date, September 28, 1985

Sharon, Lois, & Bram's Elephant Show, Season 3, Episode 34, "Soap Box Derby." Original Air Date, 1986

A Left to right: Lorne Green, Dan Blocker, Michael Landon, and Pernell Roberts after Dan Blocker won the Oil Can race, 1964

B The downtown Akron parade on the Golden Stairway at the Mayflower Hotel. *Bewitched*'s star, Elizabeth Montgomery with World Champion Bob Logan, 1966

44   How I Saw It

A Oil Can Race, top to bottom: Dale Robertson, Andy Williams, and Craig Stevens. Robertson won in a close race, 1960

B David Canary of *Bonanza* in the Oil Can Derby, 1968

C Fess Parker (top), Frankie Avalon, and Glenn Ford (bottom) in their Oil Can cars. Parker easily won the race, 1965

D Dick York, *Bewitched* star, signing autographs, 1966

1960s

How I Saw It 45

Mason Bell

Mason Bell became assistant general manager of the All-American Soap Box Derby in 1964. He was promoted to general manager in 1965. He retired from Chevrolet in 1975.

INTERVIEWER: How'd you get involved with the Derby?

BELL: In 1964, I was promoted to the national offices in Detroit as director for youth markets. My duties included the driver education program, several programs with the Jaycees and the Soap Box Derby. I had a dream job. I was busy, but it was fun.

INTERVIEWER: You must have met a lot of famous people at the Derby?

BELL: Bobby Kennedy came to the race and flagged some of the heats. He was just wonderful, completely nonpolitical. It was quite a success. Lorne Greene, from *Bonanza*, really loved the Derby. He came to the race as a visiting celebrity 5 times and even gave a fireside chat for the champs in Derby camp. John Havlicek [a former Ohio State basketball star and Hall of Fame pro for the Boston Celtics] came to the Derby a couple of years. He got so involved he wouldn't accept his fee for appearing the second and third year. We had great success with most of the celebrities. They were real human beings.

INTERVIEWER: Organizing the Derby must have been hard?

BELL: My secretary, Marie Wright, was an expert in all phases of the Derby. She was also one of the most important people ever associated with the Derby. She made sure that all of the Derby directors around the country were kept in tow. She would often help solve problems that came up. You have to remember that in those days women were given secretarial jobs, and that was it. I depended on her heavily. Wright is one of two women to be inducted into the Soap Box Derby Hall of Fame. She worked as the Derby's executive secretary from 1955 to 1972. When you're running a big event like the Soap Box Derby, you can't lose your cool. And you have to pay attention to people even if you're in a hurry.

INTERVIEWER: What did you learn running the Derby?

BELL: Carefully plan the mission, spell it out to the people, and explain fully how you want things to go. Then get out of their way and let them do it. Goodyear, Firestone, Goodrich, and General Motors had Derby representatives on a special committee. You needed a team effort to succeed. Akron had a marvelous team of people who worked on the Soap Box Derby.

How I Saw It

A John McDaniels Jr. (left) from Lynchburg, VA, raced Bobby Logan from Santa Ana, CA, in a preliminary heat. After McDaniels was declared the winner, an official reviewed the photo and determined that it was actually a dead heat. McDaniels' father demanded another review. The officials then decided that Logan, not McDaniels, was the winner. Logan went on to win the championship, 1965

B Rock Hudson behind Paul Anka (left), Arthur Godfrey, Paul Lynde, and John Russell, fighting over the Oil Can Trophy, 1963

C The German champion Lutz Aderhold thought his car would go faster if he flung himself forward at the start of the race. It had just the opposite effect. Bob Logan from Santa Ana, CA, beat him to win the championship, 1965

D Left to right: General Manager Mason Bell, World Champion Bob Logan, and Russ Fons, Assistant General Manager of the Derby, 1966

E Judy Carne from *Laugh-In* in the Derby parade, 1968

F It was 96 degrees the day that Branch Lew, with his family, earned Muncie, IN, its 4th World Champion and the last sit-up winner for 25 years, 1968

OPPOSITE PAGE The downtown parade in front of the Mayflower Hotel the day before the race, Eddy Arnold circled, 1961

1960s

How I Saw It   47

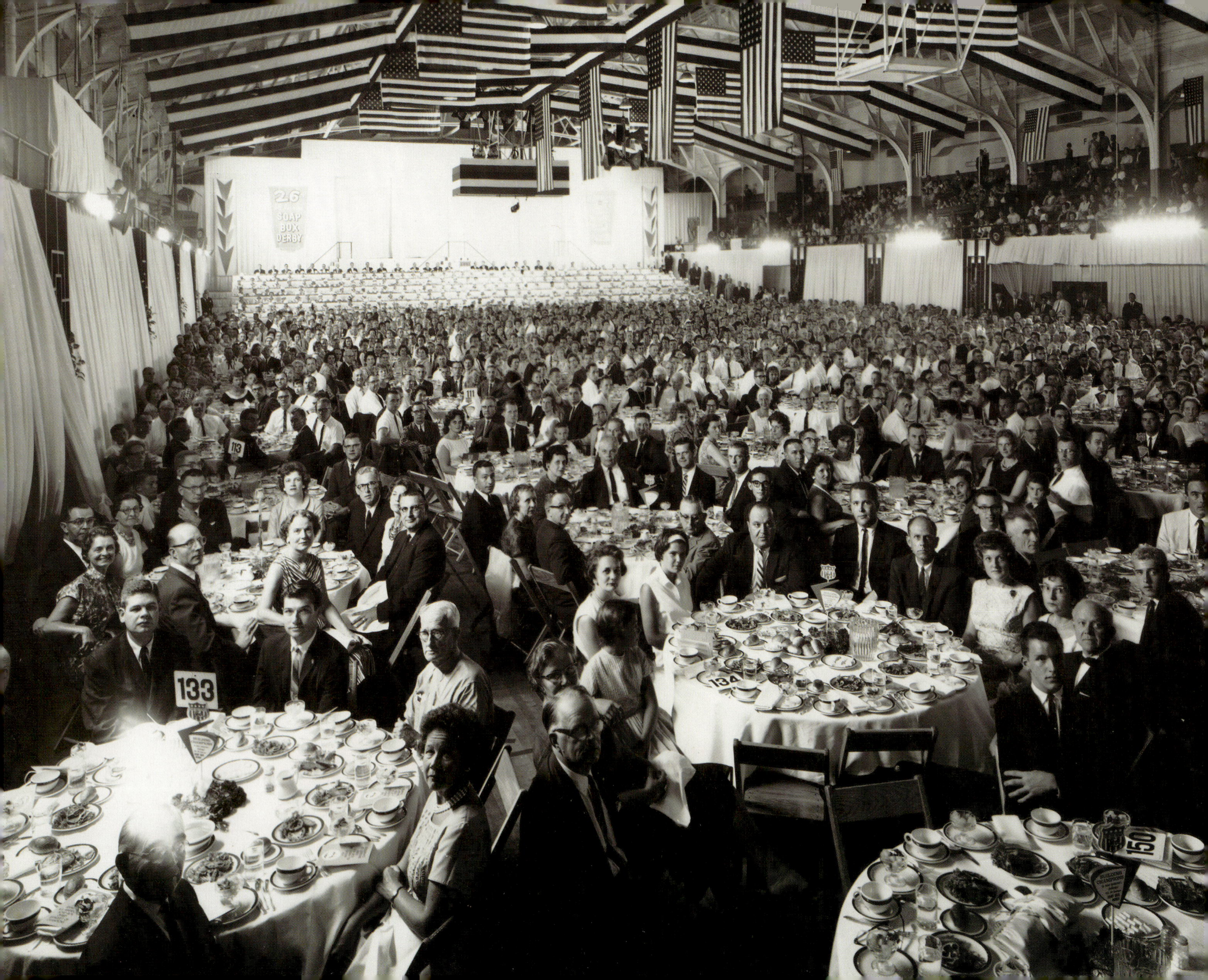
26
SOAP
BOX
DERBY
133
134
150

A The local Washington, DC Derby with Attorney General Bobby Kennedy at the start of the race, 1963

B Whitey Wahl (left) and Paul Lynde (behind), watching Rock Hudson flag the race, 1963

C & D Fans on race day, 1969

E Emmett Kelly Jr. (center) with Derby general manager, Mason Bell, and Rosemary Dunaway, America's Junior Miss, 1967. The sad-faced clown entertained the Akron crowd on several occasions, 1967

1960s

OPPOSITE PAGE All-American Soap Box Derby banquet, with approximately 3,000 attendees, 1963

How I Saw It   49

1972
ALL-AMERICAN
SOAP BOX DERBY
35
CHEVROLET
Thanks
FINISH LINE
700
500
400
300

THE 1970s
A Changing Time

The 1970s was a decade of radical change for the Derby. The all-boys event felt the wave of women's rights protests and allowed girls into the 1971 race. Newspaper interest in the Derby was waning. Cracks in the Derby's "all-American" image were beginning to show up in local races. Then, in a one-two punch, Chevrolet pulled out as the main Derby sponsor, and a cheating episode at the finals became national news. The Derby's wheels were wobbling.

1970
Soap Box Derby Season Opens with Movie Today, *Colorado Springs Gazette Telegraph*

1971
Soap Box Derby Attracts 41, *Las Cruces Sun-News (NM)*

1972
Soap Box Derby Girls Fight Custom—and Odds, *Chronicle Telegram (OH)*

1973
Cheaters Destroy Soap Box Derby, *Capital Times (WI)*

1974
Akron City Council to Fund Derby, *Times Recorder (OH)*

1975
Soap Box Derby Contest Resembles Beauty Pageant, *Delaware County Daily Times (PA)*

1976
Local Soap Box Derby is Facing Scandal, *Delaware County Daily Times (PA)*

1977
Stotts Keep It in the Family, *Galesburg Register-Mail (IL)*

1978
Kids Build Race Cars at School, *Steinbach Carillon (Manitoba)*

1979
Suit Places Two in Soap Box Derby, *Garden City Telegram (KA)*

DERBY CHATTER

Chuck Ayers

Akron's Chuck Ayers draws the popular Crankshaft *comic strip written by fellow Ohioan Tom Batiuk. Ayers previously worked as an artist and editorial cartoonist for the* Akron Beacon Journal.

INTERVIEWER: You raced in the Derby, right?
AYERS: I raced in the Derby five times and lost five times. My parents used to take me to the race when I was little. It was pretty cool. Nobody else in my neighborhood raced, but I wanted to do that. Later, my brother Mike raced, too, for three years. Mike did much better than I did. He won at least one heat every year and even won a couple of heats one year. He's always been the jock. My dad helped me some with building the car, but everything we did was within the limits of the rules. I raced in the Derby from 1959 through 1963. I loved racing in the Derby. I really did. It went beyond winning and losing. Don't get me wrong. Nobody likes to lose. I would have enjoyed winning, but I loved just going down to the basement and working on my car. Sometimes I'd spin the wheels for hours to break in the ball bearings. I was especially fanatic about that for the first several years. A trip down the track at Derby Downs takes about a half-minute. So, including my trial runs each year, my total track time for the five years I raced was maybe five minutes. That figures to just about one minute a year.

INTERVIEWER: And the drawing part?
AYERS: Even back then, I thought in pictures. I would draw pictures of Soap Box Derby racers and I would draw my car over and over again. I would design and redesign it. I even did cut-away drawings so that I knew exactly what was going on in that car. I just had the best time doing that. I remember a guy who built a car that he called The Big Cheese. The car may have been yellow. After all of these years, I'm not sure. It was the shape I remember. It was like a wedge of cheese. The guy who won the All-American in 1958, the year before I raced, was James Miley from Muncie, Indiana. He was over six foot tall. He had to double over when he raced that car. It was black with a silver stripe down the side and silver lettering. It was just beautiful. I would draw cars that I thought about building. I would make them up in my mind and then put them down on paper. I would guess that most kids probably came up with a few basic designs before building the car. Even after I had a design, I kept inventing new cars. I drew Soap Box Derby cars a lot and I'll bet that some of my homework papers had drawings of Derby cars on them, too.

INTERVIEWER: You did drawings for the *Akron Beacon Journal*?
AYERS: When I was working as an artist at the *Akron Beacon Journal*, I drew pictures of Soap Box racers for articles several times over the years. I also did a Derby painting for Chevrolet each year for about ten years. They were composite drawings with the winner's car in the center. I did that from 1966 until the year of the big cheating scandal. Chevrolet left the Derby after that.

52 *How I Saw It*

A Nancy Eichenlaub was the first girl from Akron, OH, to race. She is surrounded by a group called "Keep on Truckin" made up of 4 Akron champions and other former local Derby racers, 1971

B Akron's Chuck Ayers, the cartoonist of the popular *Crankshaft* comic strip, previously worked as an artist and editorial cartoonist for the *Akron Beacon Journal*. Each year for about ten years, he did a Derby painting like this for Chevrolet, 1971

C Joe Murphy from Beaver Falls, PA, ended up on the side rail in this first round wreck, 1976

OPPOSITE PAGE Detail from Chuck Ayers' illustration, 1971

1970s

How I Saw It 53

MY SOAP BOX

Who Really Showed for Place?

My good friend, Fred Derks, passed away in September of 2010. Fred won the All-American Derby in 1949. After his victory and since he was the third driver from Akron to win the Derby in five years, a small brouhaha ensued about Akron contestants having an advantage because they ran their qualifier on the Derby hill. The advantage never materialized. The next Akron-based winner was Craig Kitchen in 1979. Fred, who carved his Derby car out of an 80-foot walnut tree, went on to graduate from The Ohio State University with a degree in mechanical engineering. His career included a stint at Goodyear, during which he was instrumental in the construction of the Goodyear facilities in Brazil and West Virginia.

The 1949 final had a bit more controversy. The official finish-line photo shows Charles Muhl of Cleveland, OH slightly ahead of Don Klepsch of Detroit, MI. When the results got posted, Klepsch was awarded the runner-up spot and a new automobile. Muhl ended up winning a movie camera and projector. Perhaps having two kids from Ohio as the top prizes winners proved overly much for the Derby sponsors. I'm not sure, but I'm still convinced Muhl was second best that day.

A World Land Speed Holder and former Derby racer Art Arfons, special Soap Box Derby car with Novar's Tom Kilroy (right) and Jim Ott standing by. Jeff Iula is holding the front of the car, 1976

B Akron Chamber of Commerce was the main sponsor for one year, 1973

C Chevy executive, Bob Lund, awarding the world champ trophy to Larry Blair of Oroville, CA, 1971

D The first dead heat in an All-American Soap Box Derby championship. In the run-off between Joan Ferdinand from Stark County, OH, and John Pullman from Atlanta, GA, Ferdinand narrowly won. Her younger brother, Mark, won the next year. They were the first brother and sister to win the All-American championship, 1976

E Ron Reed has carved over 400 replicas of Derby cars, including the top three from each year. He was inducted into the All-American Soap Box Derby Hall of Fame in 2008, 1975

OPPOSITE PAGE Craig Kitchen of Franklin Township, OH, with the trophy he won for first place in the All-American race, 1979

1970s

How I Saw It 55

MY SOAP BOX

Crashmobiles

Matt Davis won the Zanesville local Derby in 1970. He thought the victory was "exciting" and might help him earn a scholarship so that he could become an airline pilot. Derby Downs is adjacent to Akron Fulton International Airport, so Matt's trip to the finals would put him in the driver's seat and perhaps the pilot's seat.

    Matt headed down the hill in heat 39. His car was speedy and he pulled out to an early lead. Richard Bullock, another racer in the same heat, gained speed and was about to challenge Matt. Bullock's car veered off course and into Matt's lane, striking the Zanesville car and sending both vehicles into the trackside barrier. Matt's car was totally destroyed and Richard was disqualified for racing out of his lane.

    Both boys were transported to Akron Children's Hospital. Richard ended up having muscle spasms in his back and was released. Matt's broken leg was placed in a cast. He did return to the track, and the crowd gave him a standing ovation. The elder Davis decided that it would be best to let Matt recuperate at home. Matt's race ended with a car ride back to southern Ohio instead of a chair at the post-race banquet.

(The photographs on these two pages are of the Zanesville crash.)

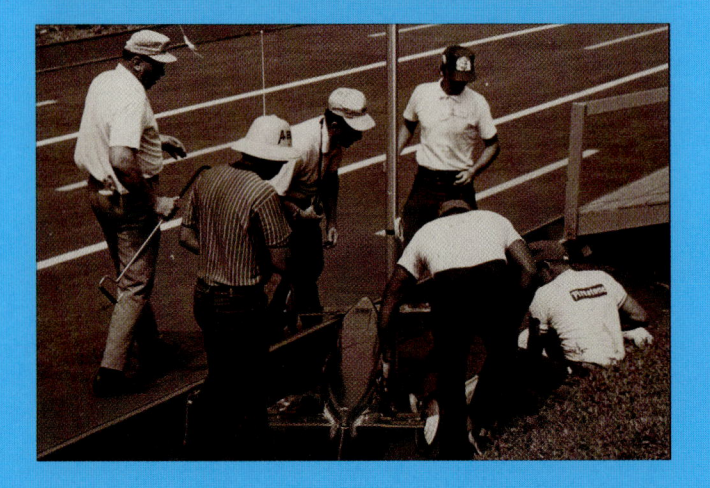

How I Saw It   57

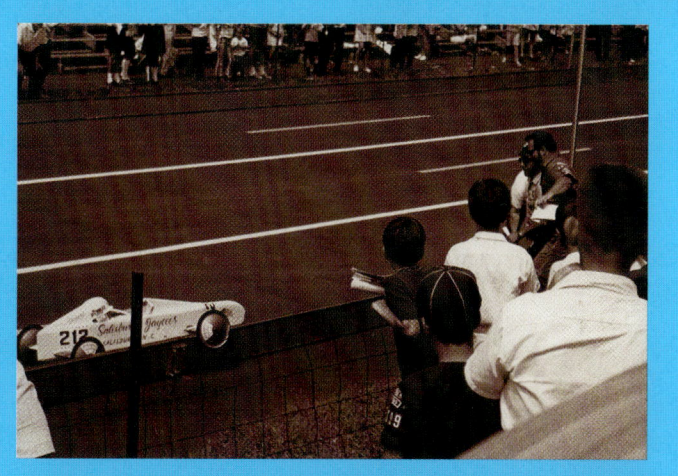

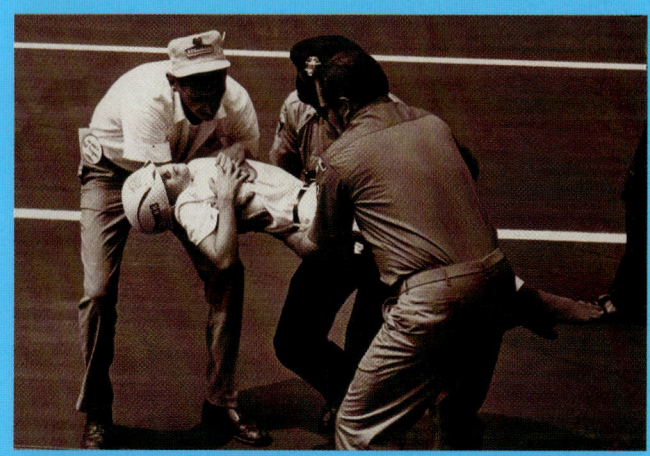

MY SOAP BOX

We Can Drive, Too!

In 1971, Gloria Steinem founded the National Women's Caucus. The same year, the first issue of *Ms.* appeared as a supplement in *New York* magazine. Newspapers included headlines like "Women's Lib Seems to Be Blooming in High Schools," "What We Should Be Doing, Sister," and "Miss America Officials Fear Women's Liberation." There was a continual cry of "Another Male Bastion Falls" when females were granted membership to previously all-male organizations.

The Soap Box Derby was caught up in the feminist tide, begrudgingly. The general manager of the Derby, A. M. Bell, sent a letter to local race organizers indicating girls should be allowed to compete "in those instances where pressure is being exerted by individuals or groups." Pressure grew across the country. Wyoming allowed girls into their local Derby and claimed to be the first state to do so.

Five girls entered the Akron local event in 1971. In 1972 Priscilla Freeman of North Carolina finished fifth, and in 1973 Diana Mills of New York came in second. Girls represent about 45% of all entrants nationwide today.

One final heat of the Derby sticks in my memory. After the three cars crossed the finish line, I heard the track announcer exclaim, "Ladies and gentlemen, we have our first girl world champ, Karren Stead." The year was 1975.

A After Chevrolet ended their sponsorship, Akron Chamber of Commerce took over as the main sponsor in 1973. With no local sponsors in many areas, many newspapers and civic organizations no longer participated in the Derby. As a result, entries fell to 138, 1972

B Novar Electronics came to the rescue of the All-American when they were running out of funds. Novar's vice-president, Tom Kilroy, is credited for coming up with the idea of sponsoring the race. The relationship lasted 13 years, 1975

C General Motors was the main sponsor for the All-American Soap Box Derby starting in 1934. They provided the final backing, the newspapers around the country provided the promotion, and the Akron rubber companies provided workers to help out at the track on race day, 1972

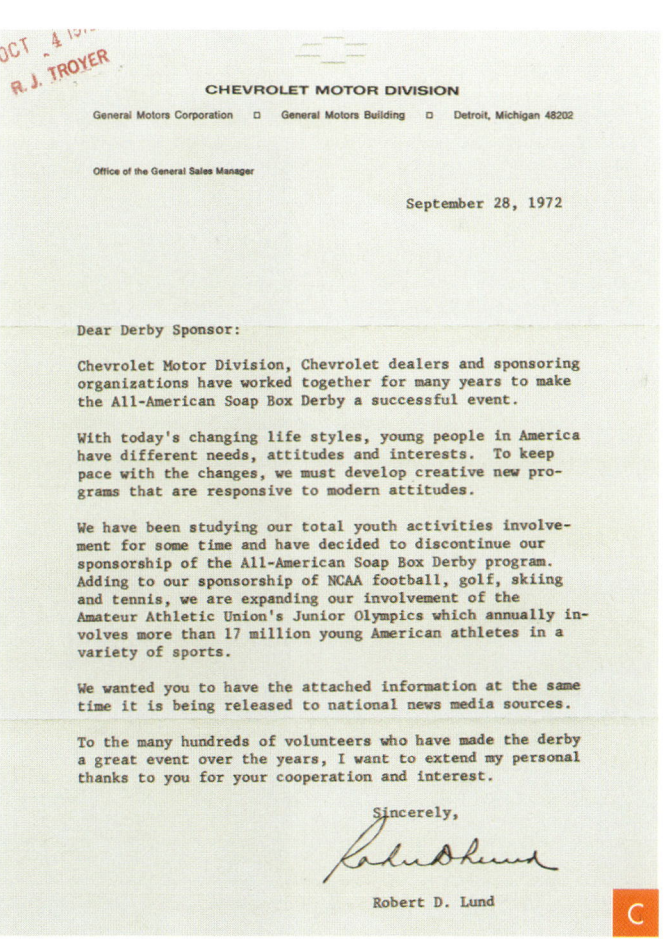

OPPOSITE PAGE Karren Stead of Lower Bucks County, PA, accepting her plaque from Bruce Buchholzer, Chairman, and F. A. "Whitey" Wahl (right), President. She was the Soap Box Derby's first female champ, 1975

1970s

How I Saw It 59

STARTING GRID

Soap Box Derby & National Derby Rallies Title Winners

Mike Burdgick

Cody Butler*

Tony Carlini*

Joel Endres*

Hilary Pearson

Kacie Rader*

Matt Wolfgang

*Won both titles in the same year

(Founded in 1977, National Derby Rallies is an organization whose goal is to allow families to become more involved in gravity-powered racing.)

60   How I Saw It

A Novar Electronics was the main sponsor from 1976 through 1988, 1978

B Joey Lunn, the 1952 Champion, returned to Akron for his car's induction in the All-American Soap Box Derby Hall of Fame, 1979

C After General Motors ended their sponsorship of the All-American, Jeff Iula (not pictured), Bobby Peel, Jimmy Underwood (1969 Akron champ), and Billy Ford (1970 Akron champ) lowered the flag to half-mast at Derby Downs, 1972

D Russ Yurk from Flint, MI, 1979 World Champion, with all his trophies. He is one of the most successful champs in history, 1982

OPPOSITE PAGE General Manager Mason Bell wanted the parade to consist of more than 100 Corvettes, with two champs riding in each. "I had a good idea what that parade would look like," Bell recalled decades later, "but I had no idea what it would sound like. The drivers revved up those Corvettes and started down the street. The kids loved it." 1970

1970s

How I Saw It   61

STARTING GRID

Cities Represented From 1936 to the Present at Every Derby

Akron, OH

Anderson, IN

Cleveland, OH

Indianapolis, IN

Cities with the Most Derby Winners

Akron, OH

Anderson, IN

Cleveland, OH

Rochester, NY

Salem, OR

A Chris Noyes from Ossining, NY, won third place in this car, 1973

B The National Derby Rallies (NDR) was started by Jerry Bryan. This is their first group of champions at their track in Warren, OH, 1977

62   How I Saw It

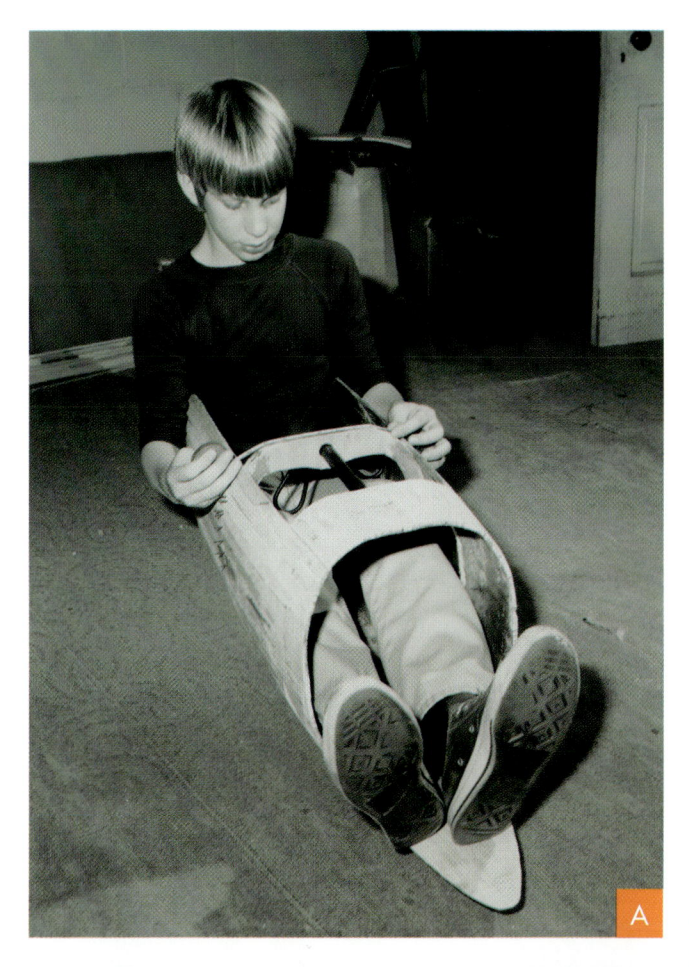

A & B 1976 World Champion Phil Raber building his car, 1977

C This wreck involving cars driven by Michael Needs from Western Nebraska, Robert Bullard from Florence, SC, and Rory Busby from Tucson, AZ, is the only three car wreck in Derby history, 1976

D Chevy's last year to sponsor. The word "Thanks" on the bridge went unnoticed until years later, 1972

How I Saw It 63

MY SOAP BOX

An Unwanted Attraction

James Gronen had a very difficult pre-Derby life. His father died when he was 8 years old, and shortly after, his mother was hospitalized with a long-term ailment. His brother and sister were sent to live with relatives in New York, and James moved in with his Colorado uncle, Robert Lange.

In the 1973 finals, Gronen's car was equipped with an electromagnet. When the metal starting gate was released, his car was "pulled" down the track. Derby officials became suspicious because Gronen's start times where quick, but his heat times got slower, which was unusual.

Gronen, the "Magnet Kid," held the All-American championship for only a few days. According to reports, Gronen was visiting his mom when the "Most-trusted Man in America," Walter Cronkite of the CBS Evening News, detailed the Derby rules violation for millions of viewers, including Gronen, who was, until then, unaware of his demise.

I contacted Gronen a few times over the years. Even as an adult, Gronen doesn't think the magnet in his racer was truly illegal. In the years that followed the Derby affair, Gronen turned to a more spiritual life, staying attached to Boulder's Naropa University, an organization that helps individuals "know themselves more deeply and engage constructively with others."

A Every serious Derby fan knows about James Gronen's 1973 well-built battery-equipped racer. Some say that he probably would have won the national race if it hadn't been for the illegal magnet hidden in his racer. Gronen says that he has spent his life seeking truth and is sorry that the scandal happened, 1973

B Driver of the "magnet car," James Gronen, waving at the crowd before he was disqualified, 1973

A Richard Decatur, winner of the Akron, OH, race, waiting for his heat to start. Today, Richard is a lieutenant on the Akron Police Department, 1975

B The car that belonged to Champion Timothy Sean McNeil from Lawton, OK, 1972

C Allen Walker, first African American champion from Akron, OH, 1972

1970s

How I Saw It   65

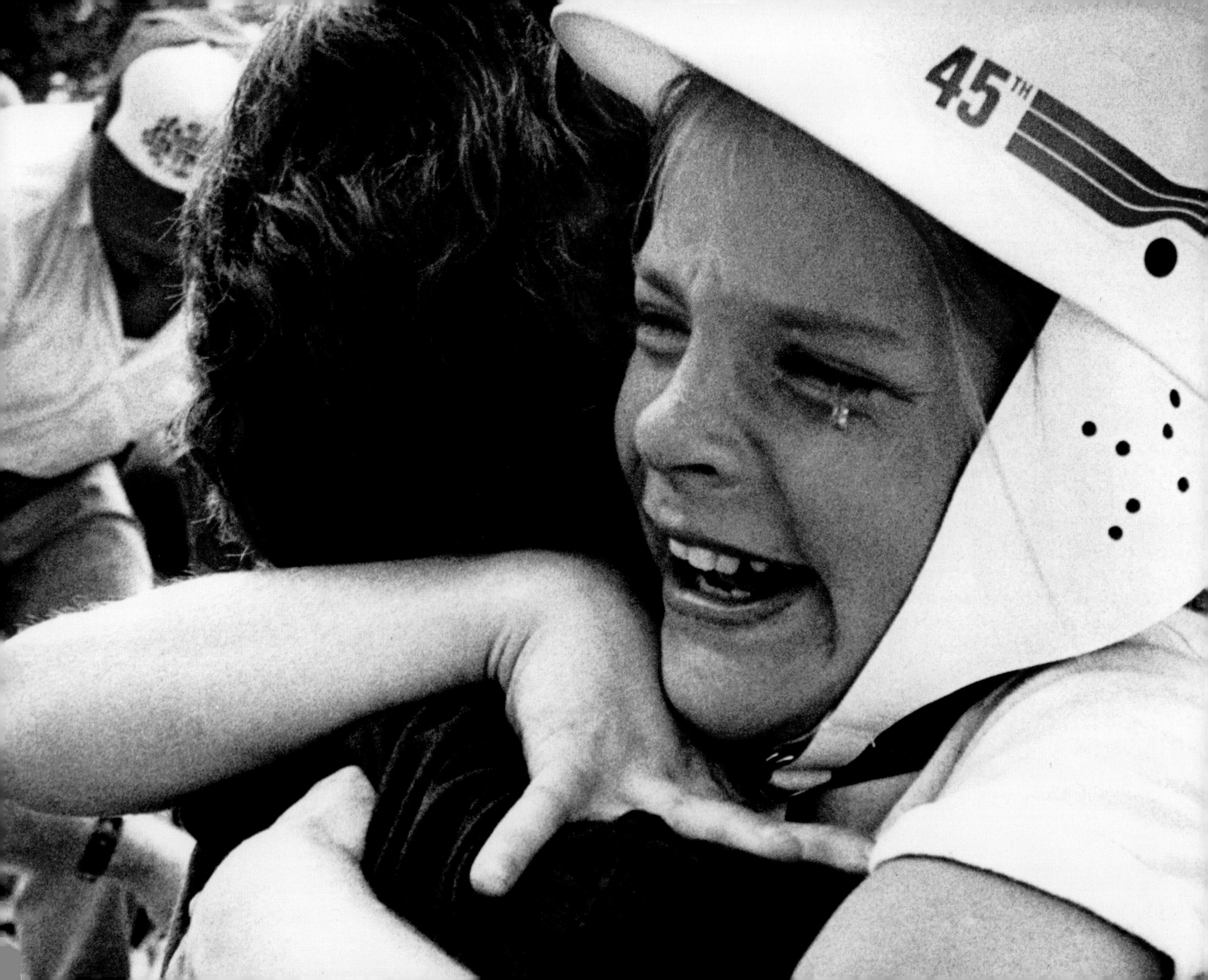
45TH

THE 1980s
Family Traditions

The Derby searched for new sponsors and the races continued. A new organization, National Derby Rallies (NDR), allowed racers other competitive venues. The All-American added new categories and crowned various champions. The Derby suffered from the lack of national media coverage. Four-wheeled vehicles still made their runs down the Derby hill, but the crowds weren't as large.

1980
Strong turnout for '80 Soap Box Derby, *Gazette* (IA)

1981
Two Indy Drivers Champs of NDR Rally, *Logansport Pharos-Tribune* (IN)

1982
The Changing Face of Syracuse: Soap Box Derby, *Syracuse Herald Journal* (NY)

1983
Parade with clowns, calliope music mark festivities at Soap Box Derby, *Gazette* (IA)

1984
Kralls dash to Derby's checkered flag, *Wisconsin State Journal*

1985
No Soap Boxes, but Derby Rolls Sunday in Bellevue, *Omaha World-Herald*

1986
Foreign participants rolling into Akron for 49th Soap Box Derby, *Orange County Register* (CA)

1987
Racers Built for 2 Soap Box Derby in Delray Adds Division for Handicapped Children, *Sun-Sentinel* (FL)

1988
'88 Soap Box Derby May Be Last for Valpo, *Post-Tribune* (IN)

1989
Solar Soap Box Derby Shines Light on Need for New Energy Technology, *Orlando Sentinel*

MY SOAP BOX

Three Champions and Me

I wouldn't be writing these stories today if it weren't for Joey Lunn. In 1982, I went to Charleston, South Carolina, to visit Joey. We decided to go for a swim. I told him I was going to swim to a sandbar that seemed pretty close. About half way out, I got tired and turned around. The undercurrent caught me. Joey, lying face down on the sand, didn't notice anything out of the ordinary. Thankfully, he heard my shouts and swam out to rescue me. Joey saved my life.

In 1939, Cliff Hardesty drew suspicion from the judges with the sophistication of his design. After being questioned by twelve committee members until midnight, he was taken to a garage the next day to duplicate the front suspension from scratch. Not only was his design legitimate, he went on to win.

I met Cliff in 1981. He told me he got some flack in 1939 because his father was a Chrysler dealer in a Chevrolet-sponsored race. Officials listed his dad as an insurance agent. I like Cliff because he stood up for himself, even as a teen.

Freddy Mohler is another good friend of mine. He has come back to Akron to watch the All-American race 49 times. He still has his trophies in the china cabinet of his house, the same house he was born in. I still get mail from Freddy and he always adds the line "1953 World Soap Box Derby Champion" after his signature. Freddy already has had his tombstone prepared with a Derby car etched onto it.

Jeff Iula

A, B, & C Parachutist Pat Kane jumped out of a plane over Derby Downs. He was to land on the track. Instead, he hit the flag pole on the bridge, which bent back and he ricocheted off on to the track, 1985

OPPOSITE PAGE 1952 World Champion Joey Lunn (left) and Scott Baio with Joey's car, 1980

How I Saw It 69

MY SOAP BOX

Big Bob Turner

I sincerely believe I love the Derby more than anyone. My wife will testify on my behalf. I admit it—I'm addicted to the Derby. I bet I'm the only man alive who could get into the *Guinness Book of Records* for talking non-stop about the Derby.

I can hear the voice of one guy, wherever he is, saying, "Hold on Jeff, we might have to duke this one out." That deep tone would be coming from Robert "Big Bob" Turner. The first national Derby champion, he continued to do as much for the race as possible until his death in 1995.

After winning in 1934, Turner returned in 1936, prompting the Derby organizers to create the Turner rule—no one who wins the top race can run in it again. That didn't stop Turner from showing up. He came to Akron for 41 straight finals. Back in Indiana, Bob sponsored kids, helped kids build cars, and even founded a Derby school to teach kids how to build, race, and win. From 1957 through 1960, the Derby champions came from Bob's school.

When I visited my family in Indiana, I regularly stopped by to see Bob. We knew each other well. Some might say Bob really did get his fill of the Derby. He weighed 525 pounds when he passed away. I was one of the 12 pallbearers who helped bury the champion.

Jeff Iula

A NASCAR Champion Dale Earnhardt Sr. taking a ride down the hill at Derby Downs in "Big Daddy," 1987

B Thirty-seven of the 61 world champs came to the banquet to celebrate the 50th anniversary, 1987

C Kit Car Champion Christopher Roberts from Indianapolis, IN, 1988

D Jeff Iula (left) and Ron Baker, the Derby general manager, 1981

OPPOSITE PAGE Bob Turner, the very first Derby champ, was named Parade Marshal at the 50th All-American race, 1987

1980s

How I Saw It   71

STARTING GRID

Talking Derby

"The banquet Saturday night was a wonderful one … They sure had some floor show." Earl Bishop, Manitowoc, WI, Champion, 1936

"It surely was a treat to get ice cream and pop anytime you wanted." Raymond Hudachek, Iowa City Champion, 1940

"Sure he had been in the hospital 4 times in the last 6 months. But, he wanted to race." Neil Hobak, whose son Doug raced in the Gary, IN, local and died of cancer the next day, 1956

"I used to make racers, just wheels and a frame, and I'd ride them down a hill." Terry Howlett, Pulaski County (VA) Champion, 1965

"Gee, Dad, why did they have to say so much about me?" Steve Gomolka, Philadelphia Champion, 1970

"[I]t was neat to meet new friends from all over the world." Chris Roseland, qualifier, Omaha, NE, 1987

"I've enjoyed (racing) because I am closer to my Dad than I originally was." Wendy Pearson, qualifier, Indianapolis, IN, 1993

"What I enjoy most is going downhill and looking out of the corners of my eyes." Coty Dietel, participant, L.A. Foothills Derby, 2003

"You have to smile and whatever happens, happens." Chelsea Buddle, participant, Danbury, CT, 2010

How I Saw It

A Carol Anne Sullivan from Rochester, NH, cries tears of joy after her victory. She was the first female to win a Kit Car championship, 1982

B Celebrities Gordon Jump, Frank Bonner, Tom Hanks, Sonny Shroyer, Eddie Mekka, Laurie Walters, and Christopher Norris with past world champions, 1981

C Tom Hanks (left) presenting a trophy to Mike Burdgick from Flint, MI, for his 7th place win. Two years later, Burdgick won the All-American in the senior division. Bill Koch on right, 1981

D World Champion Anita Jackson from St. Louis, MO, with celebrities (left to right): Brian Patrick Clarke, Dawn Parrish, Howard Morton, Lee Benton, Michael Gross, and Patricia McPherson, 1984

OPPOSITE PAGE An aerial view of Derby Downs and the Rubber Bowl, 1982

1980s

How I Saw It   73

GOODYEAR
BRIDGESTONE FIRESTONE TRUST FUND
Firestone
PEPSI
MIDAS
WARNER CABLE
GENCORP
FIRST NATIONAL BANK
AKRON Jaycees
A. Schulman Inc.
Snyder OF BERLIN
Brown Derby
GTE Mobilnet
dairy mart
The GAR Foundation
CITY OF AKRON
57th
ALL-AMERICAN SOAP BOX DERBY
1994
BUCKLE UP
RAIN-BLO
PayDay
LEAF TM
Milk Duds
JOLLY RANCHER
900
118

THE 1990s
Enduring Legacy

After two decades of instability, the Derby seemed to be finding a renewal of purpose. The Derby again was becoming the family activity it once was. Perhaps Derby administrators were adjusting to the new realities of gravity-based racing. Sponsors were stepping up to help the Akron event. At the end of the decade, the founder of the Derby passed away. Many hoped they could keep his legacy going.

1990
6th Annual Soap Box Derby Will Be Held On June 2, *Buffalo News* (NY)

1991
$5,400 Gift Keeps Soap Box Derby Rolling, *Columbus Dispatch* (OH)

1992
For First Time In 2 Decades, Soap Box Derby Day, *New York Times*

1993
Sanford Gets On Track for Soap Box Derby—The City Is Building a 775-Foot Racetrack, *Orlando Sentinel*

1994
Mobilian Wins Area's Only Soap Box Derby: Scandal-Marred Sport Making A Comeback, *Mobile Register* (AL)

1995
Far East Is Going Downhill \ Philippine Director Envisions Expansion Of Soap Box Derby Races to Other Asian Countries, *Akron Beacon Journal*

1996
Local Derby Looks to Roll Into Future, *Columbus Ledger-Enquirer* (GA)

1997
Northeast Ohio Will Get Another Hall Of Fame. This One Will Honor Soap Box Derby Greats, *Akron Beacon Journal*

1998
Obituary: Myron E. Scott, 91, Ohioan Who Created Soap Box Derby, *New York Times*

1999
PV Racers Place at First Soap Box Derby, *Pahrump Valley Times* (NV)

STARTING GRID

World Champs Come in All Sizes

Shortest   Marc Behan, 4'4"
Tallest   Jim Miley, 6'1"
Lightest   Carol Sullivan, 49 lb.
Heaviest   Garret Keyser, 165 lb.

Winning Families

Terry & Barney Townsend (Siblings)
1957 & 1959 World Champions

Bret & Curt Yarborough (Siblings)
1973 & 1974 World Champions

Joan & Mark Ferdinand (Siblings)
1976 & 1977 World Champions

Bonnie & Sally Thornton (Cousins)
1992 & 2006 World Champions

Joel & Alan Endres (Siblings)
1994 & 1999 World Champions

Jamee & Amy Clemens (Siblings)
1994 & 2002 World Rally Champions

Ashley & Dennis VanFossen (Siblings)
2001 & 2007 World Rally Champions

How I Saw It

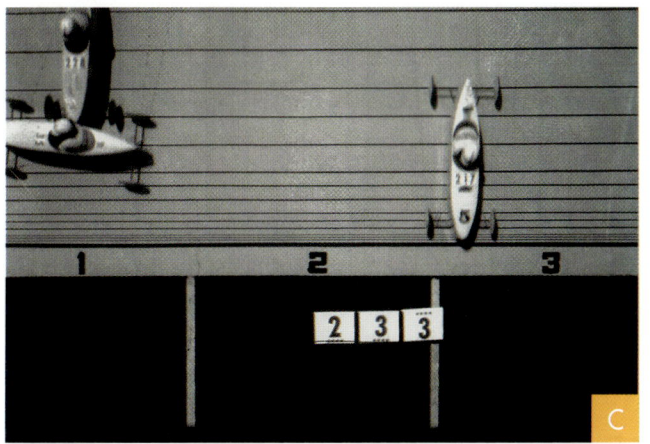

A The first All-American winner, Bob Turner, was so proud of his accomplishment that he had it etched on his grave stone, 1995

B The University of Akron's mascot, Zippy, with 1987 champion and university cheerleader, Heather Seabeck, 1995

C Claudia Garcia from Houston, TX, crashed into Anthony Medlock from Flushing Meadow, NY. Ryan Harrison from Columbia, MS, was declared the winner, 1994

D Three cars stopping in the Midas breaking area beyond the finish line, 1994

E Indy Rookie of the Year, Lyn St. James (back), with 3 World Champs—Bonnie Thornton (Masters), Carolyn Fox (Kit Car), and Loren Hurst (Stock), 1992

F Ross Mallinger, sitting in a replica of the first winner's car, and celebrities, from left to right, Thomas Nicholas, Robert Gibson, Leslie Easterbrook, Tony Dow, Leanza Cornett, and Tom Sneva, 1993

OPPOSITE PAGE National Derby Rallies Sit-Up National Champion Kelly Dughi, 1998

1990s

How I Saw It   77

Rule Changes

1934	Only year that was handicapped
1948	Graphite was no longer allowed
1948	Windshields were banned
1949	The use of power tools was disallowed
1953	Vertical steering was banned
1964	Racers were allowed to lie backwards in their car
1965	Lead and steel were allowed as building materials
1971	Girls were allowed to race
1972	Shotgun steering not permitted
1973	Calibrated wheels were required
1976	Required use of standard kits, race was divided into two divisions
1981	Fiberglass shell kits introduced
1986	Rally program introduced
1992	Stock division created
1994	Kit division dropped and Super Stock division introduced
1999	Fiberglass model name "Scottie" introduced
2000	The "Scottie" became mandatory

A Teresa Oles, a local Champion from Chicago, IL, with the dog, Spuds MacKenzie. Spuds MacKenzie was also famous for her Bud Light commercials, 1991

B In 1981, the first Super Kids Classic race was held in Akron, OH. Other local races were held throughout the country. In 2003, the National Super Kids Classic held their first race in Akron, OH, on the same track as the All-American Soap Box Derby, 1995

C Derbytown champs at the celebrity luncheon. Over forty percent of the racers were girls by then, 1996

D A reunion of four previous champions with Jeff Iula. Terry Townsend (1957), Jeff, Joey Lunn (1952), David Mann (1962), and Kenny Cline (1967), 1992

E Michael Delorenzo, unidentified woman, Jon Provost, Julie St. Claire, Robert Reed, John Andretti, and Jim Donovan after Oil Can race, 1991

OPPOSITE PAGE When Novar decided not to continue as the national sponsor, it recruited First National Bank, which went on to sponsor the race from 1989–1992, 1992

1990s

How I Saw It   79

MY SOAP BOX

The Soap Box Hall of Fame

Let's just say Myron "Scottie" Scott walked his own path. Some people even thought he was a bit crotchety. He wasn't thrilled about the Derby's 1971 decision to let girls compete. Scottie had strong opinions about a lot of topics, including the manly sports car. After all, he gave the Chevy Corvette its moniker.

In 1987, I got the idea to start a Derby Hall of Fame. Canton, Ohio had the Football Hall of Fame, and the Derby had been around about as long as professional football. I talked to the Derby board about the options, but it took about a decade to plead my case before I got the go-ahead.

In 1997, I convinced Derby founder, Myron E. Scott, to come back to be enshrined in the Derby Hall of Fame. My idea was to induct the "S" class—Myron E. Scott, Bain E. "Shorty" Fulton (instrumental in building Derby Downs), Jim Schlemmer (*Akron Beacon Journal* Sports Editor who helped get support from local tire companies for the Derby), Jimmy Stewart, and Wilbur Shaw.

Scottie and his bride of 70 years, Clara Jane, came up from Kettering, Ohio. They stayed at the Quaker Hilton Hotel for the weekend. Scottie was the parade marshal and he graciously signed autographs for a bevy of people. He told me he was thrilled to be back. "I'm ninety-years old and I have all these pretty girls around me."

Jeff Iula

80

A Ralph Iula was inducted into the All-American Soap Box Derby Hall of Fame by his son, Jeff Iula (a 2006 inductee), 1999

B Loris Troyer and his son, Bob Troyer (a 2003 inductee), when he was inducted into the All-American Soap Box Derby Hall of Fame, 1999

C Akron's Kelly Dughi, 8th place winner, with family. Kelly holds the record for most trips down Derby Downs—851 times, 1993

D This letter from President Ford was printed in the program, 1997

OPPOSITE PAGE Myron Scott (left) and Jeff Iula at the 60th anniversary race, 1997

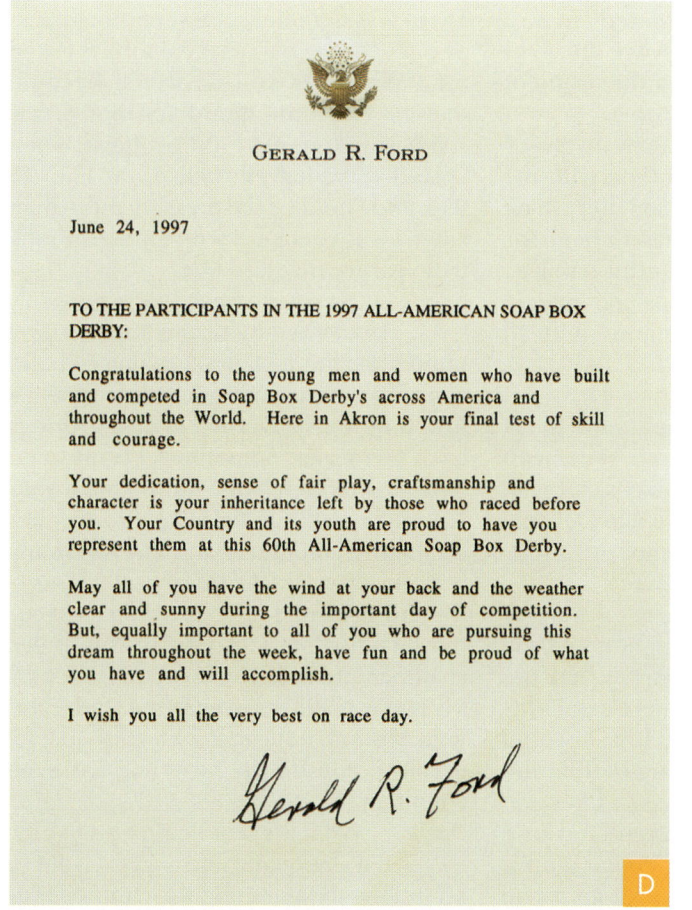

GERALD R. FORD

June 24, 1997

TO THE PARTICIPANTS IN THE 1997 ALL-AMERICAN SOAP BOX DERBY:

Congratulations to the young men and women who have built and competed in Soap Box Derby's across America and throughout the World. Here in Akron is your final test of skill and courage.

Your dedication, sense of fair play, craftsmanship and character is your inheritance left by those who raced before you. Your Country and its youth are proud to have you represent them at this 60th All-American Soap Box Derby.

May all of you have the wind at your back and the weather clear and sunny during the important day of competition. But, equally important to all of you who are pursuing this dream throughout the week, have fun and be proud of what you have and will accomplish.

I wish you all the very best on race day.

Gerald R. Ford

1990s

How I Saw It   81

Danielle Del Ferraro

Danielle Del Ferraro, now Danielle Hier, is the only two-time champ in All-American Soap Box Derby history. She won the 1993 Kit Car and the 1994 Masters championship.

INTERVIEWER: As with many Derby entrants, your dad lent a hand.

DANIELLE: My dad was a perfectionist. He made cabinets and was a trim carpenter. When it came to my car, everything had to be done neat and clean with attention to the details. He taught me that this would help make it go faster. I remember sanding and sanding and sanding the car. Since it was going to be painted anyway, I sometimes wondered why we did all of that work. We even sanded the *inside* of the car.

INTERVIEWER: Was your whole family involved?

DANIELLE: Yes. I got to spend time with my family. We went to places that I don't think I'd have ever gone to if it hadn't been for the Derby. I met other Derby families, hung out with other champs and made a lot of friends. It was just a good time all around.

INTERVIEWER: And at home?

DANIELLE: People at my school knew that I was a Soap Box Derby champ. When you came into town, there were signs that said: "Stow, Ohio, Home of Danielle Del Ferraro, Two-time World Champ."

INTERVIEWER: Did you feel pressure?

DANIELLE: Racing should be fun. I never got uptight about it. I was uptight about my grades and the sports I was in, but the Derby was just fun. I had a relaxed attitude about it. Even if I had lost, it would have still been fun. Winning is all in the driving. Concentrate, focus, and keep in mind that every track is different. You have to learn those differences. Preparation is important, too. Those cars are very small and you have to be flexible. I remember stretching all the time. The race where I won the masters championship was very close. The videotape showed that I drove pretty much in a straight line. The girl who came close to beating me swerved all over the way down the track. It's easy to get off track when rolling down the hill, especially when it's windy. Since I was just out to have fun, it was easy for me to focus. There was definitely pressure though, especially the second year. Reporters asked me, "What will you do if you become the first two-time World Champ?" I was still having fun, but I did get tense when I raced in the Rally in 1996. I was 15 or 16 then and I noticed the pressure more than when I was younger. I won the Derby rally that year for my third title.

INTERVIEWER: Do you go back to the track?

DANIELLE: Yes. When I visit the track today, I remember the feeling of zoning out and concentrating as I was going down the hill. Any time I visit Derby Downs, it brings back memories. Sometimes I want to go back down the hill one more time just to remember what it feels like. I remember the Derby volunteers and Pat Taylor, my regional director. He was always supportive and helpful. I also remember executive director Tony DeLuca and Bob Troyer, chairman of the Derby Board of Directors. My family is still involved in the Derby and we go to watch the races. My husband, Al, usually comes to the races and has even volunteered.

INTERVIEWER: What are you doing now?

DANIELLE: I'm a neonatal nurse now. I went to school for six years, and the Derby scholarships helped out.

A Sami Jones of Salem, OR, stenciled "Singin Sami" on the side of her car as part of her strategy. She figured that musical vibrations might help her win the race, so she sang and hummed as she went down. She won first place at the All-American that year, 1990

B Jeff Iula and Jon Provost, star of the *Lassie* TV series, 1991

C World Champion James Marsh from Cleveland, OH, shows off his car and trophy, 1998

D The first Stock Car World Champion, Loren Hurst from Hudson, OH, 1992

OPPOSITE PAGE The only two-time World Champion in history, Danielle Del Ferraro from Stow, OH, 1994

How I Saw It 83

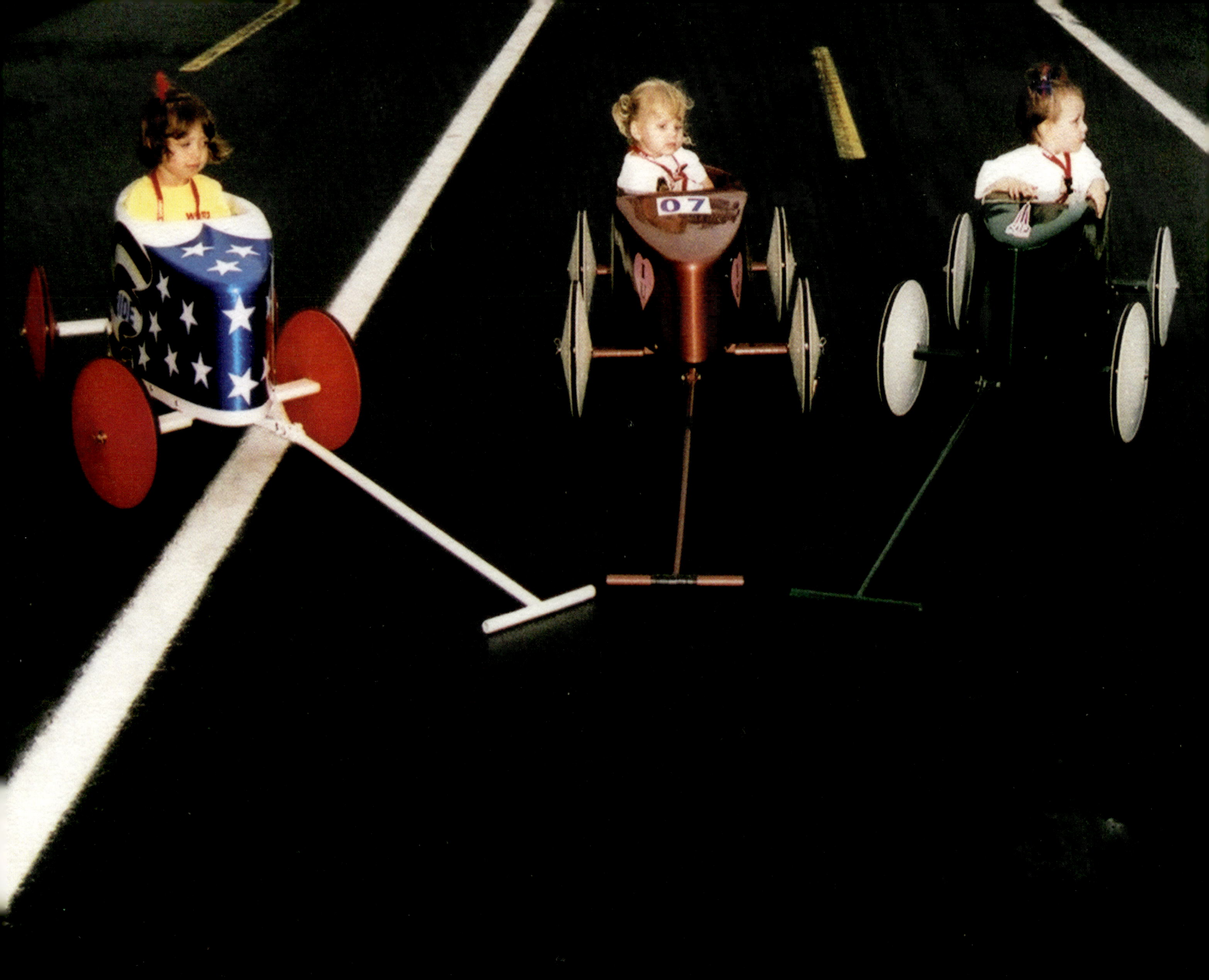
07

THE 2000s
The Need for Tradition

Despite another cheating event in 2003, the Derby regained participants and interest. In a world filled with digital gadgetry, maybe there was a valued place in American hearts for the simplicity of the Derby. By the end of the decade, the Derby organization made internal changes which caused strife. More importantly, however, the U.S. financial crisis made funding almost impossible and sponsorships barely available. Other alternatives were needed to keep the wheels turning.

2000
Grant Provided to Purchase Soap Box Derby Cars, Rio Rancho Observer (NM)

2001
Soap Box Derby: Disney Movie Creates New Interest in Youth Sport that Runs On Steep Roads, Ventura County Star (CA)

2002
Cousins Win Red Cross Soap Box Derby, Jackson Citizen Patriot (MI)

2003
Soap Box Derby Champ Stripped of Title, Sun Herald (MS)

2004
Volunteers Connect Chicago Kids With Soapbox Racing Excitement, Daily Herald (IL)

2005
Soap Box Derby Enjoys Revival, Houston Chronicle

2006
Chance to Enter Adult 'Soap Box' Derby, Hot Springs Village Voice (AR)

2007
Special Day at the Races—Special Needs Children Teamed With "Pro-Drivers" in Bucks County's First Soap Box Derby for Special Needs Kids, Intelligencer (PA)

2008
Cub Scouts to Hold Soap Box Derby, West Milford Messenger (NJ)

2009
After Almost 20 Years, Locals Try to Get the Auburn Funk Soap Box Derby Rolling Once Again, Auburn Journal (CA)

The Bologna Train

Since all Derby finalists had won local derbies, the Derby organizers treated each racer who came to Akron as a true winner. All entrants usually received wristwatches and a few other items of memorabilia, including their racing helmets. Of course, in the gravy years of well-heeled sponsors, banquets, hotel accommodations, parades, and other activities were never an issue. The post-Derby banquet, during which the winners were given their grand prizes, was a lavish event filled with pomp and circumstance.

In 2007, NASCAR left the Derby, and a new sponsor could not be immediately identified. The Derby needed to economize. After asking Derby families about pre-race events, a big picnic was held at an Akron park so Derby entrants and their parents could mingle and socialize. The day was to include games, hot dogs, hamburgers, and fun. Well, somehow either too many people showed up or too few hot dogs and hamburgers were ordered. When I got there, some people were complaining about standing in line. Maybe it was just pre-race jitters. Then, I saw what was at the end of the line—bologna sandwiches. Champs were chomping on white bread and cold cuts. We had come a long way. Maybe we needed some new steering lessons.

A World Rally Champions, left to right: Masters, Alexis Rhodes from Conneaut, OH; Super Stock, Zak Boll from Stow, OH; and Stock, Koby Garnhart from Winnebago, IL, 2003

B Derby Downs on race day, 2002

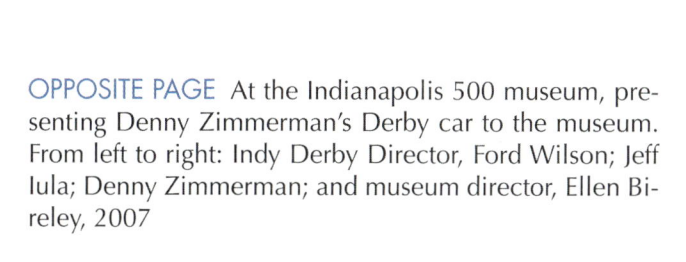

OPPOSITE PAGE At the Indianapolis 500 museum, presenting Denny Zimmerman's Derby car to the museum. From left to right: Indy Derby Director, Ford Wilson; Jeff Iula; Denny Zimmerman; and museum director, Ellen Bireley, 2007

How I Saw It 87

DERBY CHATTER

Ron Reed

Retired steel worker, Ron Reed, has carved miniature pine replicas of every winning All-American Soap Box Derby racer from 1934 to the present.

INTERVIEWER: How do you make the replicas?
REED: I don't measure anything. I just look at a picture of the Derby car I want to carve and start whacking away. I started carving the 1935 Derby cars that had run in the national race because I think they're more interesting than modern cars. Those old cars were much more varied in their styles and shapes, and the wheels weren't standardized. A lot of them had bicycle wheels back then. Today the cars look pretty much alike since they're all built from a kit. In the early days, they came in a lot of different shapes and sizes.

INTERVIEWER: You must have been to a lot of races?
REED: I'm not positive, but I think I hold the record for the most All-American races attended. I've been to 60. I went to my first Derby race in 1949. My uncle and my dad took me that year. I've missed only three races since then. The only one who might have gone to more races is Whitey Wahl, former President of International Soap Box Derby and the 1999 inductee into the Soap Box Derby Hall of Fame. When Chevy handled the race in the old days, it was a big deal. The crowds were huge and you had to stand for every heat that an Akron driver was in or you couldn't see anything. The crowd was always on its feet when the hometown kids went down the hill. When the drivers were announced, you couldn't hear anything that was said. The crowd made that much noise. It was exciting. Another thing that still stands out in my mind is radio announcer Alan Jackson. The local Akron radio announcer, Harold Hageman, described the action all day long until the final heat when Alan Jackson of CBS took the microphone. When he took over he said, "This is Alan Jackson, and I'm in Akron, Ohio at the bottom of the hill. This is not just any hill. This is Derby Downs!" There's no other sound in the world like a Derby car coming down the hill on steel wheels. You wouldn't call it a rumble, but it's definitely the sound of the bearings in the wheel that you hear. It's hard to describe, but when you hear it, you know what it is!

OPPOSITE *Ron Reed has carved over 400 replicas of Derby cars, including the top three from each year, 1975*

How I Saw It

A Race day Parade of Champions, 2000

B Tony DeLuca, Executive Director, and Jeff Iula, General Manager, ran the Derby from 1989–2009. They expanded the program from 160 champs to almost 500, 2007

C Mason Bell (right) presenting Jeff Iula with a plaque for 30 years of service to the Derby, 2005

D Champions' cars on display pre-race, 2004

E Reunion of the 1951 final heat, from left to right, Ray Marconi, Darwin Cooper, and Paul "Fred" Albright, with Jeff Iula, 2001

How I Saw It   89

MY SOAP BOX

I Part Ways with the Derby

The Soap Box Derby has been a huge part of my life. After volunteering at Derby Downs for 13 years, I went to work full-time for the race. It was my dream job. After more than 35 years of being around the drama, charm, and friendship of the Derby, I am pursuing other paths.

I'm now a councilman-at-large in Cuyahoga Falls, Ohio, just up the road from Akron. My Derby years will probably provide me with some guidance in the political realm. The topics might change, but committee meetings still seem the same.

The Derby is facing an uphill battle at this point. I hope the new Derby CEO, Joe Mazur, will lay out a plan to provide sound footing for the event. Kids just naturally like to compete, and racing in the Derby provides a positive experience. Parents who help their children and grandchildren, like I am doing, can establish a good basis for future communication and problem-solving.

Corbin Bernsen, who played Roger Dorn in *Major League,* heard about the Derby problems and decided to do something to help. He came to Akron to shoot a film about the Derby, *25 Hill*. A percentage of the profits will go to the Derby.

I still love the Derby and keep abreast of what's going on. It's hard to close a chapter of my life that takes up so many pages. I hope the Derby will start to gain momentum again, just like the cars at the top of the hill!

Jeff Iula

A Leading the way in the pre-race rain parade are future champs Trinity Kubick and Abby Postlethwait, pulled by Nancy Iula (left), Trinity's grandmother, and Patty Postlethwait (right), Abby's mother. Levi Strauss sponsored the race from 2005–2007, 2006

B World Champion Megan Evans from Kansas City, MO. Megan placed three times in All-American competition, 2000

C Akron police officers, Summit County sheriff's deputies, and the Akron Fire Department are always on hand for the All-American, 2002

OPPOSITE PAGE Bob Troyer presenting the All-American Soap Box Derby Hall of Fame plaque to Jeff Iula, 2006

How I Saw It   91

STARTING GRID

Local Participants Who Became Race Professionals

Chris Economaki—Indy 500 Announcer

Pat O'Brien—CBS Announcer

Bobby Olivero

Swede Savage

Tom Sneva—1983 Indy 500 Champion

George Snider

Cale Yarborough

Denny Zimmerman—The only person to race in the National Derby Finals and the Indy 500

Fathers and Sons Inducted into Hall of Fame

Ralph and Jeff Iula

Loris and Bob Troyer

How I Saw It

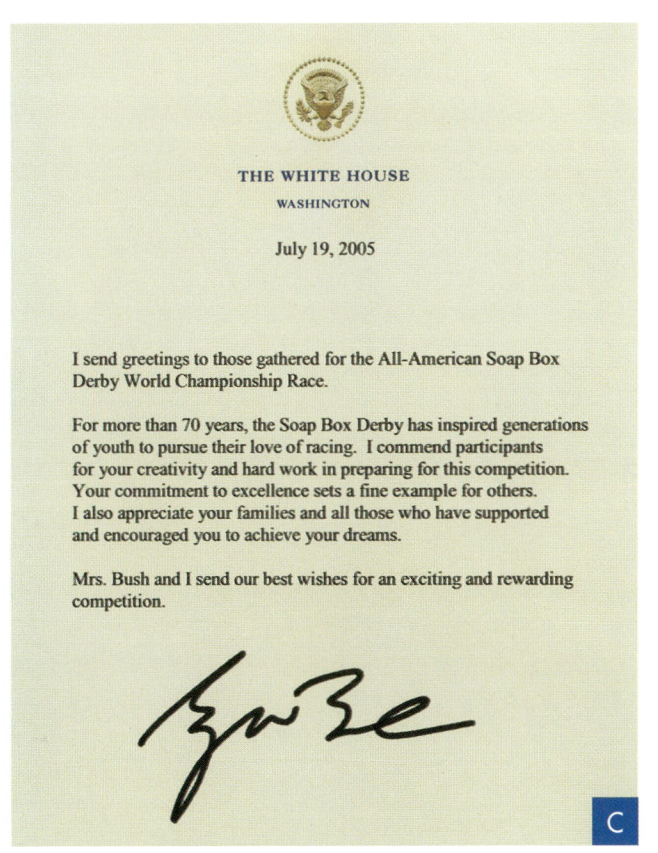

A Derby mascot, Ducky Downs, with Carrie Kubick and her children, Zoe and Trinity (right), 2006

B Appearing on an N.P.R. radio show, Jeff Iula (left) and the 2005 World Champion, Tyler Gallagher of Portage County, OH, 2008

C This letter from President Bush was printed in the program, 2005

D The Derby was without a sponsor from 1995 to 1997. From 1998 to 2002, Goodyear was the main sponsor, 2000

OPPOSITE PAGE From 2003 to 2004, Home Depot was the main sponsor of the All-American, 2004

THE WHITE HOUSE
WASHINGTON

July 19, 2005

I send greetings to those gathered for the All-American Soap Box Derby World Championship Race.

For more than 70 years, the Soap Box Derby has inspired generations of youth to pursue their love of racing. I commend participants for your creativity and hard work in preparing for this competition. Your commitment to excellence sets a fine example for others. I also appreciate your families and all those who have supported and encouraged you to achieve your dreams.

Mrs. Bush and I send our best wishes for an exciting and rewarding competition.

How I Saw It   93

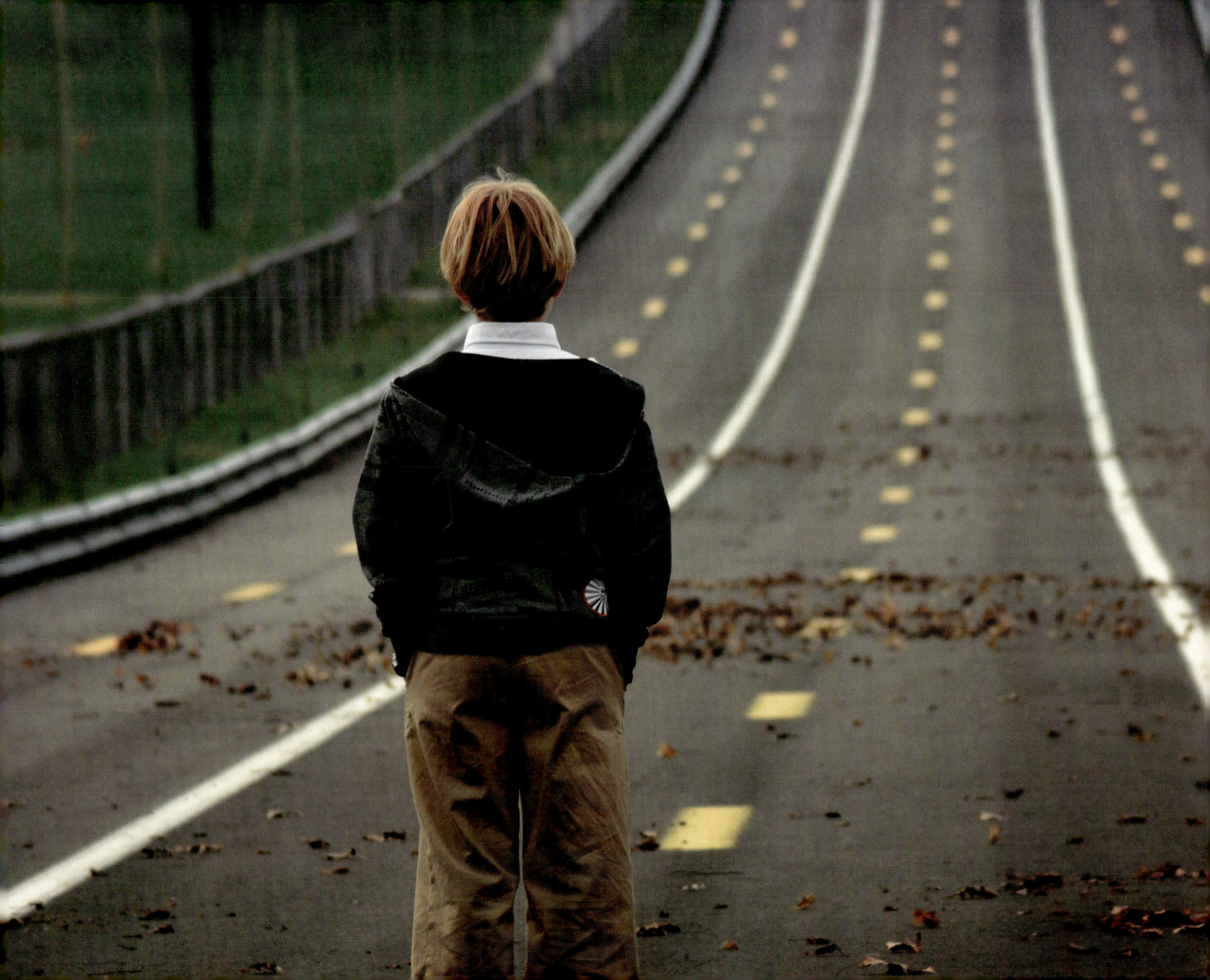

2010
Today's Race

After reading a September story in *USA Today* about the financial difficulties of the Akron-based All American Soap Box Derby, actor, director, and producer Corbin Bernsen decided he could do something to save the nearly 75-year-old youth racing league—and keep it in Akron. Despite a record number of racers (ages 8–17), the Derby lost money three out of the past five years.

The *USA Today* story inspired Bernsen to write a screenplay about a 12-year-old boy whose Derby dreams are threatened, first when his father is killed fighting in Afghanistan, and then when money troubles shut down the Derby. The Derby is ultimately saved, but that heroic role has been left open—purposely—to be filled by the real-life rescuers, the new title sponsor who comes to the Derby's aid.

THE MAKING OF 25 HILL

A Nathan Gamble driving his car past the stands at Derby Downs during the filming, 2010

B Dennis VanFossen, 2007 Super Stock Rally champion, in Derby car and Nathan Gamble, 2010

C Director, Corbin Bernsen, 2010

96 *How I Saw It*

A Corbin Bernsen with videographer, 2010

B Ralph Waite surrounded by fans at Derby Downs, 2010

C Jeff Iula, on right, offering driving tips to a driver during the filming of *25 Hill*, 2010

How I Saw It   97

SCENES FROM 25 HILL

A Nathan Gamble at his father's grave, 2010

B Nathan Gamble in his Derby car, 2010

C Nathan Gamble, star of *25 Hill*, 2010

D Corbin Bernsen, Nathan Gamble, and Maureen Flannigan, 2010

How I Saw It

CARS
The Driving Force

Fifty thousand boys entered local races to qualify for the National Soap Box Derby final in 1936. In that year, cars came in all sizes and varieties. Restrictions were not that stringent—the car couldn't weigh more than 175 pounds and the materials to build the vehicle had to cost $10 or less. Kids could use parts from a variety of sources, and even someone's garbage could be turned into Soap Box Derby gold.

As the race evolved, the Derby itself began to sell car kits for all of the racing divisions—they wanted to ensure that everyone was starting from the same point. The kits currently cost up to $500, plus an additional $100 for the Z-Glas racing wheels. In a small way, the race became professionalized.

Estimating the number of Derby cars built since the Dayton start is futile. Some inventions probably didn't even make it to the first heat of a local qualifier. Cars have come in all colors and from places near and far. Now they all have four wheels, go down the track three abreast, and only one ends up as the best.

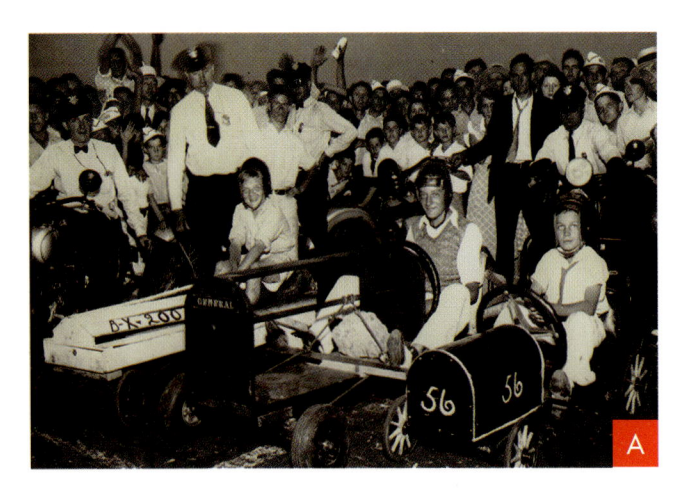

A Dick Moosbrugger in car 200, an unknown contestant, and Myron E. Litherland in car 56, waiting to start the race, 1934

B In the first All-American race in Dayton, OH, blocks were used to hold back the cars at the starting line. Ray Kern from Indianapolis, IN, won that heat, 1934

C This car is thought to be one of the best built cars in the history of the Derby. It was built by Jack Furstenberg of Omaha, NE. He placed 3rd because the final heat was handicapped, 1934

D Left to right: Harold Hansen from White Plains, NY, Loney Kline from Akron, OH, and Earl Mossiman from Minneapolis, MN, 1935

E This car was raced in the Indianapolis, IN, local race, 1935

100   How I Saw It

A John Tabor of Pittsburgh, PA, won design and construction trophies for his car, 1936

B Jack Thompson from Minneapolis, MN, showing his car to a race official, 1937

C Robert Holland from St. Paul, MN, receiving good luck wishes from a Derby official, 1937

D "Mushroom" car (right) driven by Walter Johnson from Sioux City, IA, 1937

E Louis Adams from Petoskey, MI, having his car's weight checked before the race, 1937

How I Saw It   101

A Herbert Herrmann, the first champion from Hawaii, taking a break with another racer, 1938

B Cliff Hardesty from White Plains, NY, in his car at the starting line. Fifty-two letters of protest arrived at Derby headquarters before Cliff Hardesty showed up in Akron. Each of the writers was certain that he did little or nothing in the building of his car, 1939

C James Miley (left) from Muncie, IN, winner of the world championship, David Hilligoss from Anderson, IN, and Ronnie Ashley (right) from Los Angeles, CA, 1958

D Douglas Falcon won the most unusual design award for this car in the Akron, OH, local race, 1957

102 How I Saw It

A Barney Townsend from Anderson, IN, won, even with a broken collar bone, 1959

B One of the first real sleek sit-up cars driven by Jim Kordon from Akron, OH, 1960

C Vince Rubino, in his silver anniversary helmet, won the best brake award for this car, with his father, 1962

How I Saw It

A Kirk Murphy drove this car nicknamed "The Coffin" in the Akron, OH, local race, 1967

B Racer from Cleveland, OH, in a local race, 1967

C Kenny Cline from Lincoln, NE, World Champ, started the race in this car, 1968

D A view of the interior of car built by David West from Tacoma, WA, 1968

E Champion Michael Cobb from Amarillo, TX, in his lay-down car, 1969

How I Saw It

A The winner of 6th place, Quentin Thomas from Richmond, IN, in his car called "Ironing Board," 1969

B Marion F. Cauhape from Carlsbad, NM, 1970

C A lay-down car, a lean-forward car, and a sit-up car. The orange sit-up car driven by Ken Underwood from Akron, OH, won the heat, 1970

D Billy Ford's car, which is one of the last old style sit-ups to win the Akron, OH, local race, 1970

How I Saw It   105

A A fast lay-down driven by Kim Kirby from Spartanburg, SC, 1971

B Joseph Frank Tully from Norfolk, VA, had to reach his hands over his shoulders to steer the car, 1971

C Champion Dale Wallace Brainard from Salem, OR, 1971

D Derek Fitzgerald from Augusta, GA, in his lay-down car, which placed 7th in the All-American Derby, 1977

How I Saw It

A Jeff Townsend won the senior division in the Anderson, IN, race. His father, Barney, winner of the 1959 All-American Derby, passed away just three weeks before Jeff won his local race. Jeff was trying to win in a car called "Dad's Dream." He lost to World Champ Steve Washburn of Bristol, CT, 1977

B Steve Frechino from Empire State, NY, drove this elaborately painted car, 1978

C Bruce Schlegel from Shelby, OH, 1978

D Stuart Paul from Hamilton, OH, won an award for the best designed car the year he raced, 1979

E Final heat when Danny Purol from Northern California beat Beth Frye from Dayton, OH, (middle), and Tim Jones of the Mid-West Open (IN), for the title, 1980

F World Rally Super Stock Champion, Zak Boll from Stow, OH. His grandfather, Bill Ford Sr., helped design the super stock car, 2003

How I Saw It   107

Memorabilia
The Stuff of History

Every large event with a long history produces additional materials that are collectibles—programs, buttons, flags, banners, and posters. The Soap Box Derby has had its share of other items, including Derby glasses, pins, toy car sets, and even a Hummel figurine.

Some folks trade or sell their Derby items. Others collect them. Some simply look at them and remember the charm of the event. Taken together, these items provide an archaeology of the event. A dig through sites like eBay or an estate sale can open up a new view of the Derby. A dusty remnant might reveal a fascinating story about a competitor or race. The use of certain words in an older program or advertisement might shed light on the times.

109

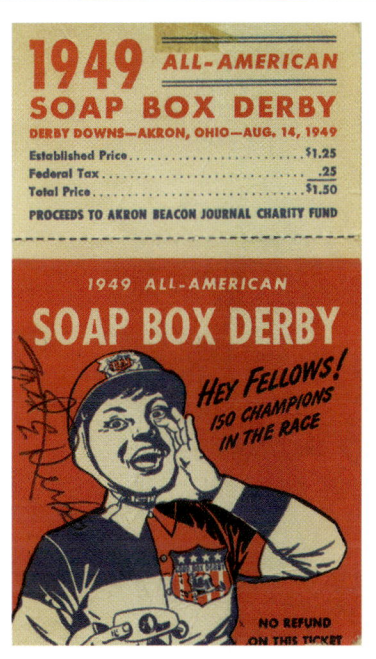

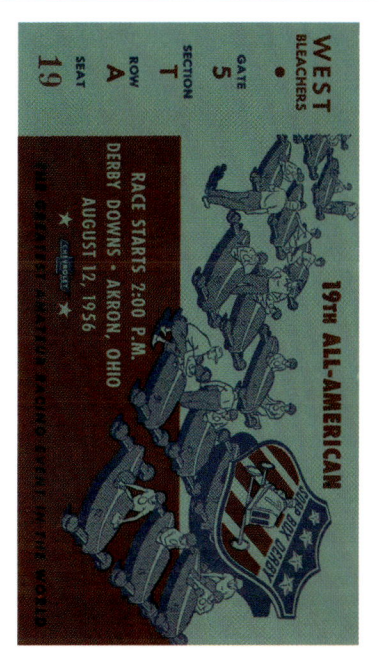

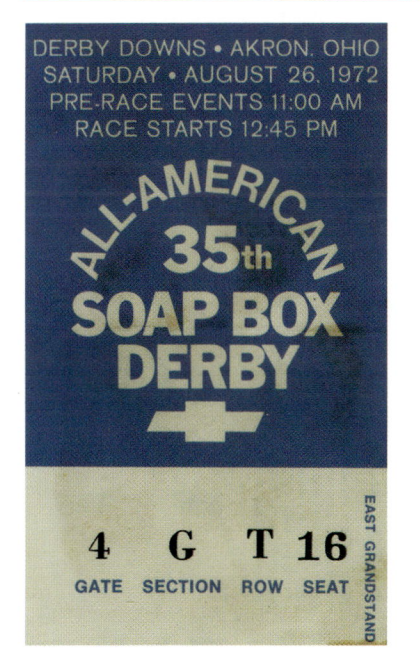

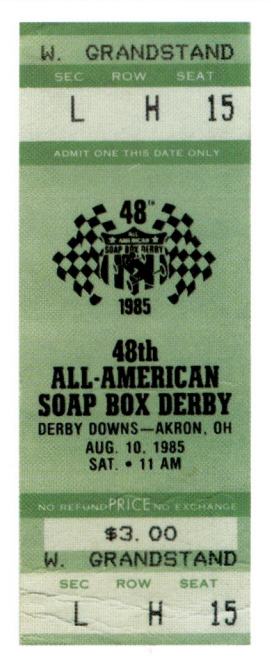

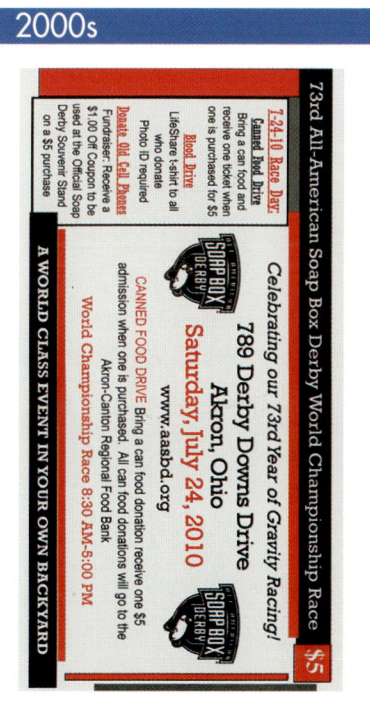

PROGRAMS AND RULE BOOKS

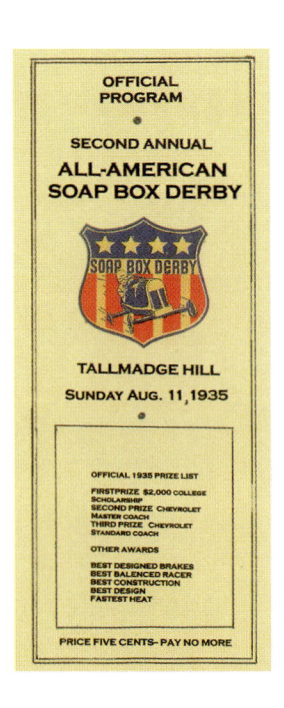

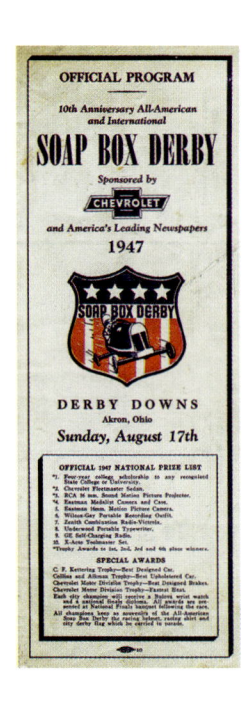

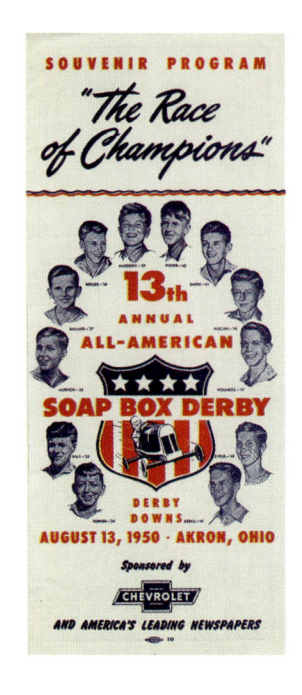

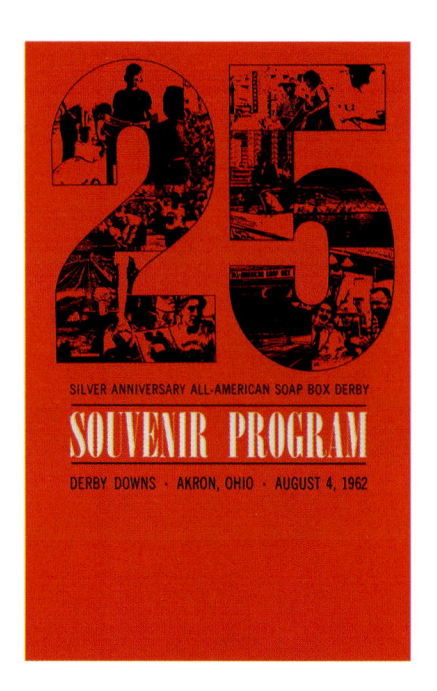

1930s | **1940s** | **1950s** | **1960s**

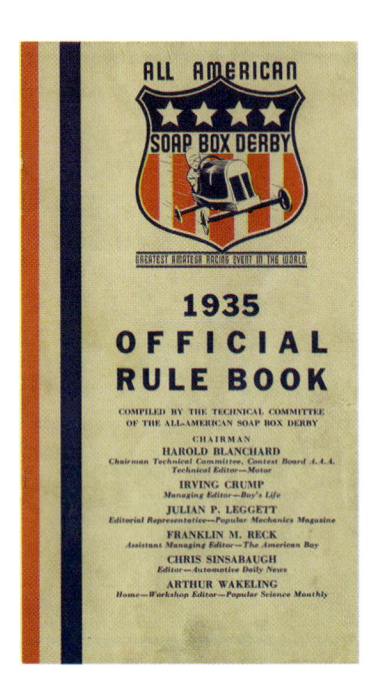

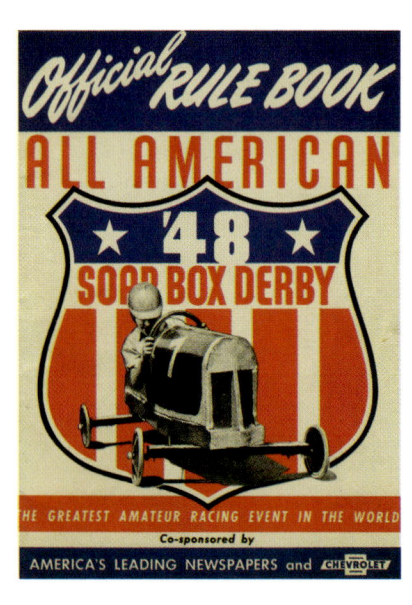

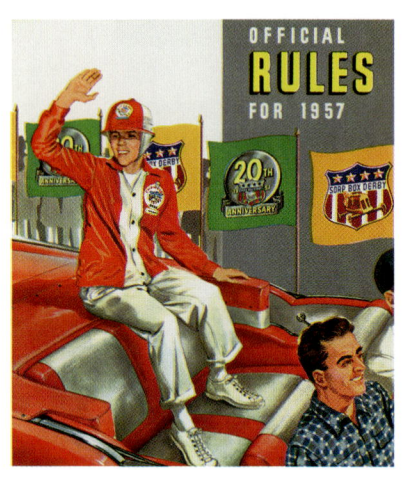

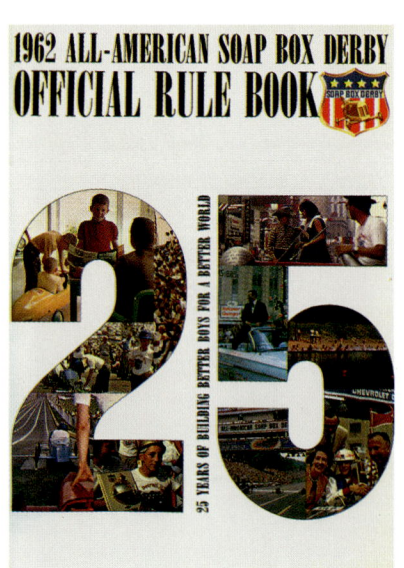

110

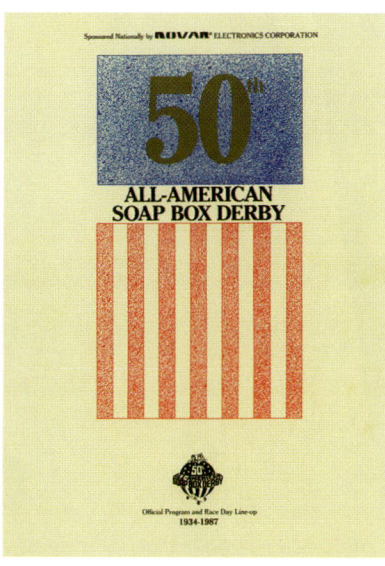

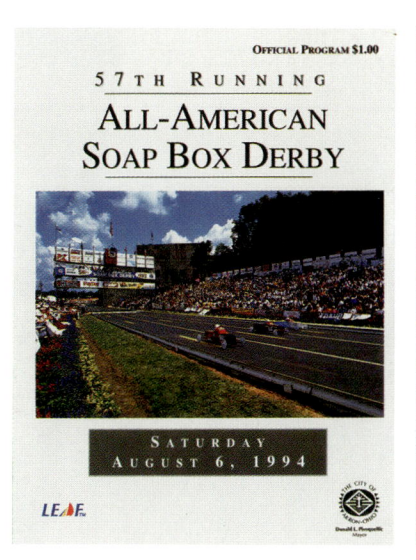

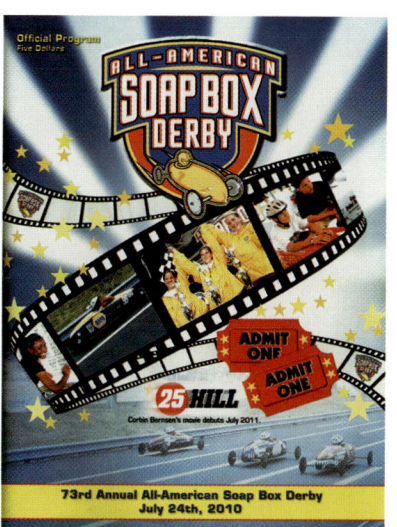

| 1970s | 1980s | 1990s | 2000s |

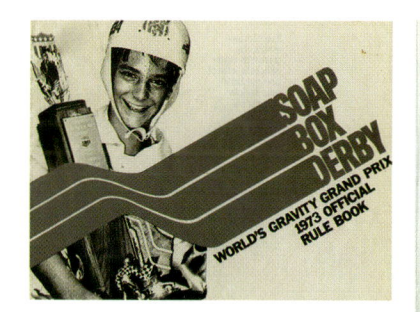

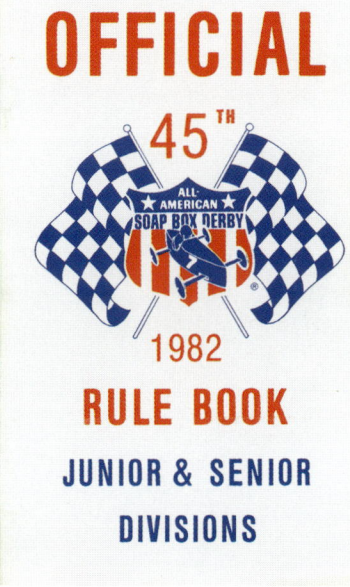

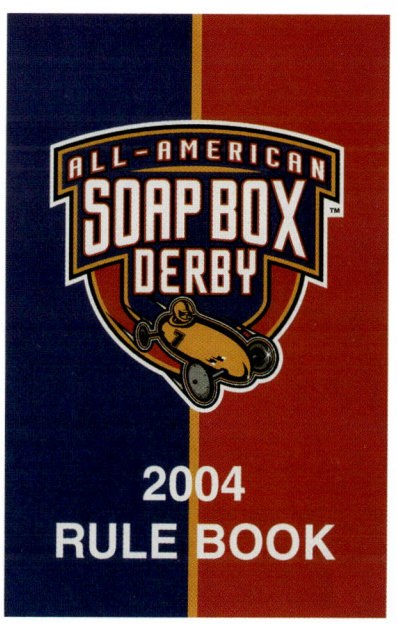

111

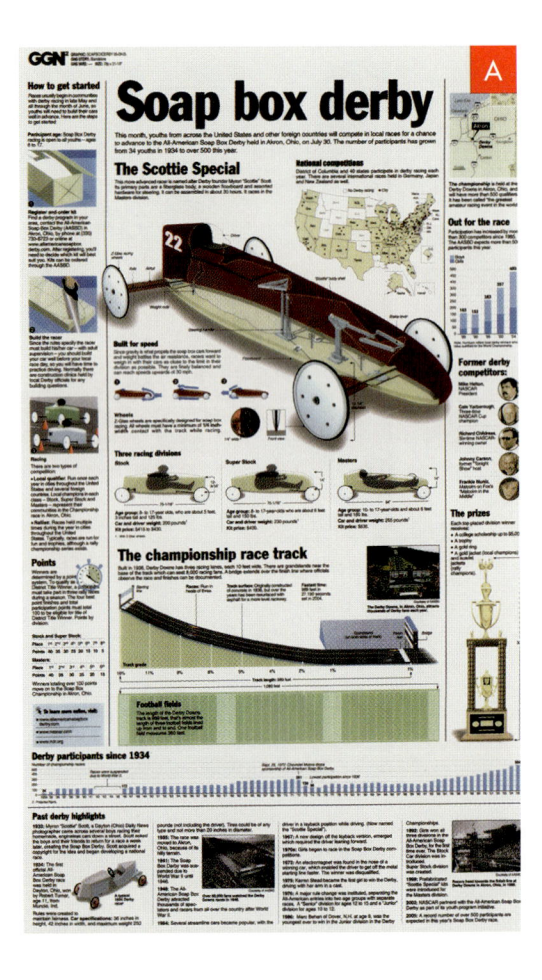

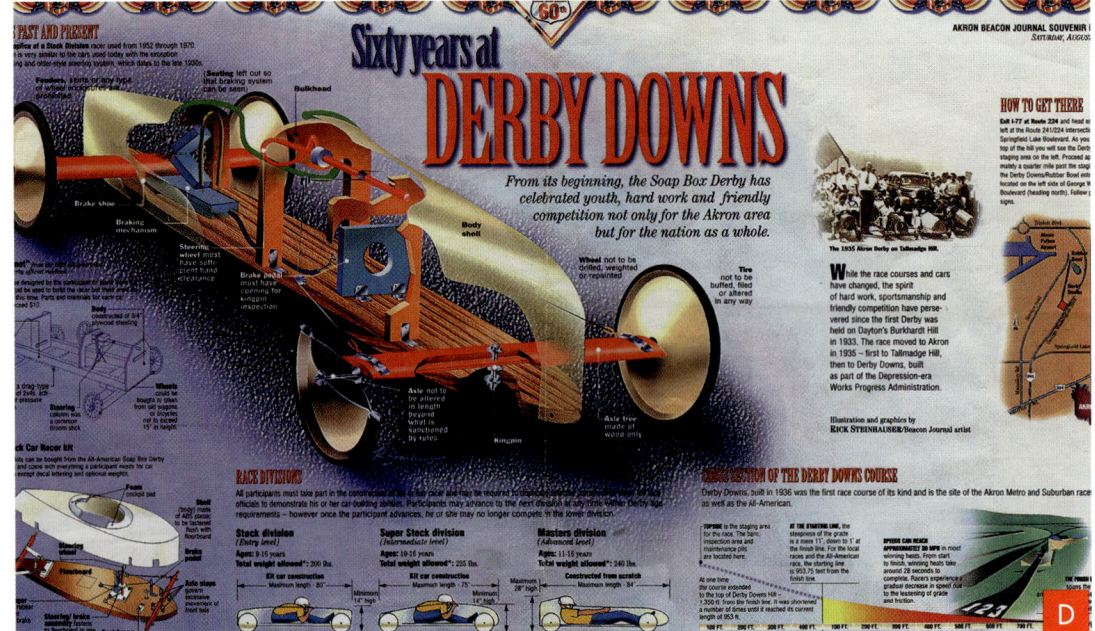

IN PRINT

A Insert in *USA Today* on June 9, 2005

B Official Derby pennant

C Ad from March 1968 issue of *Boys' Life*. Carson lost to the boy who would become the 1938 national champ, Bobby Berger of Nebraska City, NE

D "Sixty years at Derby Downs" appeared as a commemorative poster in the *Akron Beacon Journal* on August 9, 1997

OPPOSITE PAGE Insert in the *Akron Beacon Journal* on August 11, 1989

112

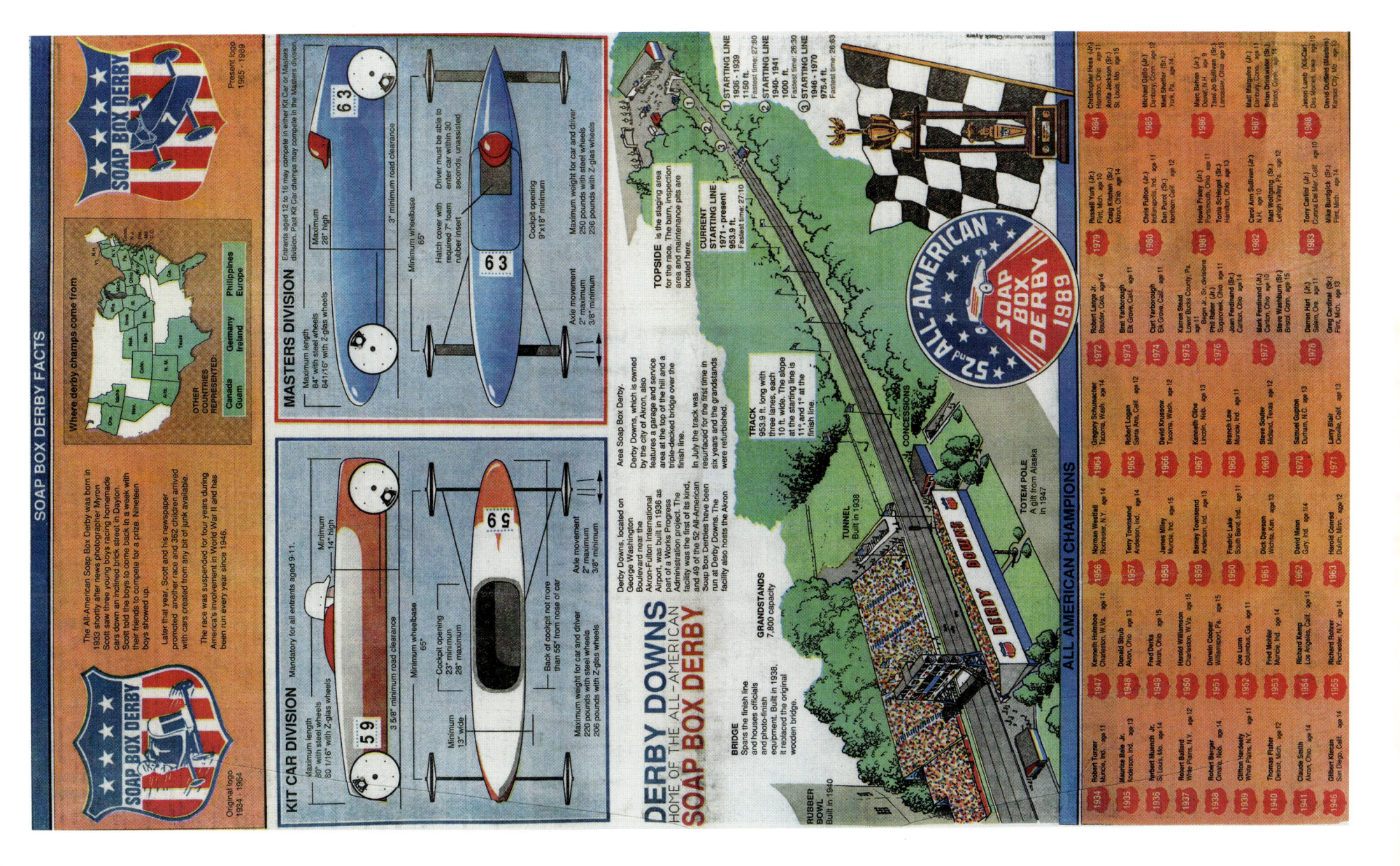

SOAP BOX DERBY FACTS

Original logo 1934-1964
Present logo 1965-1989

The All-American Soap Box Derby was born in 1933 shortly after news photographer Myron Scott saw three young boys racing homemade cars down an inclined street in Dayton. Scott told the boys to come back in a week with their friends to compete for a prize. Nineteen boys showed up.

Later that year, Scott and his newspaper promoted another race and 362 children arrived with cars created from any bit of junk available.

The race was suspended for four years during America's involvement in World War II and has been run every year since 1946.

Where derby champs come from

OTHER COUNTRIES REPRESENTED:
Canada, Germany, Philippines
Guam, Ireland, Europe

KIT CAR DIVISION
Mandatory for all entrants aged 9-11.

- Maximum length: 80" with steel wheels, 80 1/16" with Z-glas wheels
- Minimum 14" high
- 3 5/8" minimum road clearance
- Minimum wheelbase 65"
- Cockpit opening 23" minimum, 28" maximum
- Back of cockpit not more than 55" from nose of car
- Minimum 13" wide
- Axle movement 2" maximum, 3/8" minimum
- Maximum weight for car and driver: 220 pounds with steel wheels, 206 pounds with Z-glas wheels

MASTERS DIVISION
Entrants aged 12 to 16 may compete in either Kit Car or Masters division. Past Kit Car champs may compete in the Masters division.

- Maximum length: 84" with steel wheels, 84 1/16" with Z-glas wheels
- Maximum 28" high
- 3" minimum road clearance
- Minimum wheelbase 65"
- Driver must be able to enter car within 30 seconds, unassisted
- Hatch cover with required 7" foam rubber insert
- Cockpit opening 9"x18" minimum
- Axle movement 2" maximum, 3/8" minimum
- Maximum weight for car and driver: 250 pounds with steel wheels, 236 pounds with Z-glas wheels

DERBY DOWNS
HOME OF THE ALL-AMERICAN SOAP BOX DERBY

Derby Downs, located on George Washington Boulevard near the Akron-Fulton International Airport, was built in 1936 as part of a Works Progress Administration project. The facility was the first of its kind, and 49 of the 52 All-American Soap Box Derbies have been run at Derby Downs. The facility also hosts the Akron Area Soap Box Derby.

Derby Downs, which is owned by the city of Akron, also features a garage and service area at the top of the hill and a triple-decked bridge over the finish line.

In July the track was resurfaced for the first time in six years and the grandstands were refurbished.

BRIDGE Spans the finish line and houses officials and photo-finish equipment. Built in 1938, it replaced the original wooden bridge.

GRANDSTANDS 7,800 capacity

RUBBER BOWL Built in 1940

TUNNEL Built in 1938

TOTEM POLE A gift from Alaska in 1947

TOPSIDE is the staging area for the race. The barn, inspection area and maintenance pits are located here.

TRACK 953.9 ft. long with three lanes, each 10 ft. wide. The slope at the starting line is 11° and 1° at the finish line.

① STARTING LINE 1936-1939 1150 ft. Fastest time: 27:80
② STARTING LINE 1940-1941 1000 ft. Fastest time: 25:50
③ STARTING LINE 1946-1970 975.4 ft. Fastest time: 26:63

CURRENT STARTING LINE 1971-present 953.9 ft. Fastest time: 27:10

52nd ALL-AMERICAN SOAP BOX DERBY 1989

Beacon Journal/Chuck Ayers

ALL AMERICAN CHAMPIONS

Year	Champion
1934	Robert Turner, Muncie, Ind. age 11
1935	Maurice Bale Jr., Anderson, Ind. age 13
1936	Herbert Muench Jr., St. Louis, Mo. age 14
1937	Robert Ballard, White Plains, N.Y. age 12
1938	Robert Berger, Omaha, Neb. age 14
1939	Clifton Hardesty, White Plains, N.Y. age 11
1940	Thomas Fisher, Detroit, Mich. age 12
1941	Claude Smith, San Diego, Calif. age 14
1946	Gilbert Klecan, San Diego, Calif. age 14
1947	Kenneth Holmboe, Charleston, W.Va. age 14
1948	Donald Strub, Akron, Ohio age 13
1949	Fred Derks, Akron, Ohio age 15
1950	Harold Williamson, Charleston, W.Va. age 15
1951	Darwin Cooper, Williamsport, Pa. age 13
1952	Joe Lunn, Columbus, Ga. age 11
1953	Fred Mohler, Muncie, Ind. age 14
1954	Richard Kemp, Los Angeles, Calif. age 14
1955	Richard Rohrer, Rochester, N.Y. age 14
1956	Norman Westfall, Rochester, N.Y. age 14
1957	Terry Townsend, Anderson, Ind. age 14
1958	James Miley, Muncie, Ind. age 15
1959	Barney Townsend, Anderson, Ind. age 13
1960	Fredric Lake, South Bend, Ind. age 14
1961	Dick Dawson, Wichita, Kan. age 14
1962	David Mann, Gary, Ind. age 14
1963	Harold Conrad, Duluth, Minn. age 14
1964	Gregory Schumacher, Tacoma, Wash. age 12
1965	Robert Lagan, Santa Ana, Calif. age 11
1966	David Kruskov, Tacoma, Wash. age 12
1967	Kenneth Cline, Lincoln, Neb. age 13
1968	Branch Lew, Muncie, Ind. age 11
1969	Steve Souter, Midland, Texas age 12
1970	Samuel Gupton, Durham, N.C. age 14
1971	Darren Hart, Salem, Ore. age 13
1972	Larry Blair, Oroville, Calif. age 14
1973	Robert Lange Jr., Boulder, Colo. age 14
1974	Bret Yarborough, Elk Grove, Calif. age 11
1975	Curt Yarborough, Elk Grove, Calif. age 12
1976	Phil Raber, Sugarcreek, Ohio age 13
1977	Joan Ferdinand (Sr.), Canton, Ohio age 11
1978	Mark Ferdinand (Jr.), Canton, Ohio age 12
1979	Russell Yurk (Jr.), Flint, Mich. age 10
1980	Chris Fulton (Jr.), Northern Calif. age 14
1981	Howie Fraley (Jr.), Portsmouth, Ohio age 11
1982	Carol Ann Sullivan (Jr.), N.H. age 10
1983	Tony Carlini (Jr.), Eureka Del Mar, Calif. age 14
1984	Christopher Hess (Jr.), Hamilton, Ohio age 11
1985	Michael Giffin (Jr.), Danbury, Conn. age 12
1986	Marc Behan (Jr.), Donald St. Jr.-Baltimore, Ohio age 13
1987	Matt Bilgrein (Jr.), Lancaster, Ohio age 13
1987	Brian Drinkwater (Sr.), Bristol, Conn. age 14
1987	Matt Wolfgang (Sr.), Lehigh Valley, Pa. age 15
1988	Mike Burdgick (Sr.), Des Moines, Iowa age 15
1988	Jason Lamb (KitCar), Kansas City, Mo. age 10
1988	Steve Washburn (Sr.), Bristol, Conn. age 15
1988	David Duffield (Masters)

113

POSTERS

A Cal Winebrenner created this poster for the Derby's 60th anniversary, 1997

B WVIZ/PBS ideastream© and Bridgestone Corporation poster for the live telecast of the movie, *Soap Box Derby: An All-American Classic*, 1991

114

How I Saw It
My Life With the Derby

This section is truly mine. These pictures tell the story of how the Derby has crossed over into my personal life. I guess I never did erect a boundary between Derby Downs and my life. Perhaps I have the special Derby gene, passed down to me from my father. Maybe I have gotten my Doctorate in Derby Doings, and can relate quite well to those who care about the race like I do. Maybe I just feel the excitement each summer when the Derby gang returns to Akron.

People call me "Mr. Derby." I am a known quantity. I am also a family man and an average guy with a passion for gravity-based racing and boxes of Derby paraphernalia. That ain't so bad now, is it?

A Me after I took my trial run in the car owned by Raymond Rapoza who couldn't make it to Akron because of an airline strike. Billy Ford on the left and Jay Iula on the right, 1966

B My first Derby car with my cousin, Bob Baynes (right), 1957

C I proposed to my future wife, Nancy, backstage at the Derby awards show at The University of Akron's E. J. Thomas Hall. After she accepted, Bruce Buchholzer called us on stage to share the news, 1989

D My wedding party included several Derby champions, 1990

E Chris Roberts (left), Indianapolis champion, with me, his uncle, 1988

116 *How I Saw It*

A I'm standing behind my sister Jerri Roberts and her family. She is pictured with her husband Gary, and children Courtney, Chris, and Matt. Matt (foreground) won the local Indianapolis Derby in 1992. Chris won the local Indianapolis Derby in 1988, 1992

B My daughter Kelly Dughi raced in the All-American 5 times in her car and once as a substitute driver. She placed 3 times, 1999

C My daughter Carrie Cole raced 3 years in local races. She never won a heat but did win 2 phases, 1991

D The third generation of the Iula family to race. My granddaughter Trinity Kubick placed 8th in the Akron local and went on to the All-American in 2011, 2010

E Dick Goddard, winner of the 2007 Oil Can Derby, 1946 Akron local racer, and Channel 8 weatherman, and me, 2007

How I Saw It   117

MYRON E. SCOTT
8/12/97

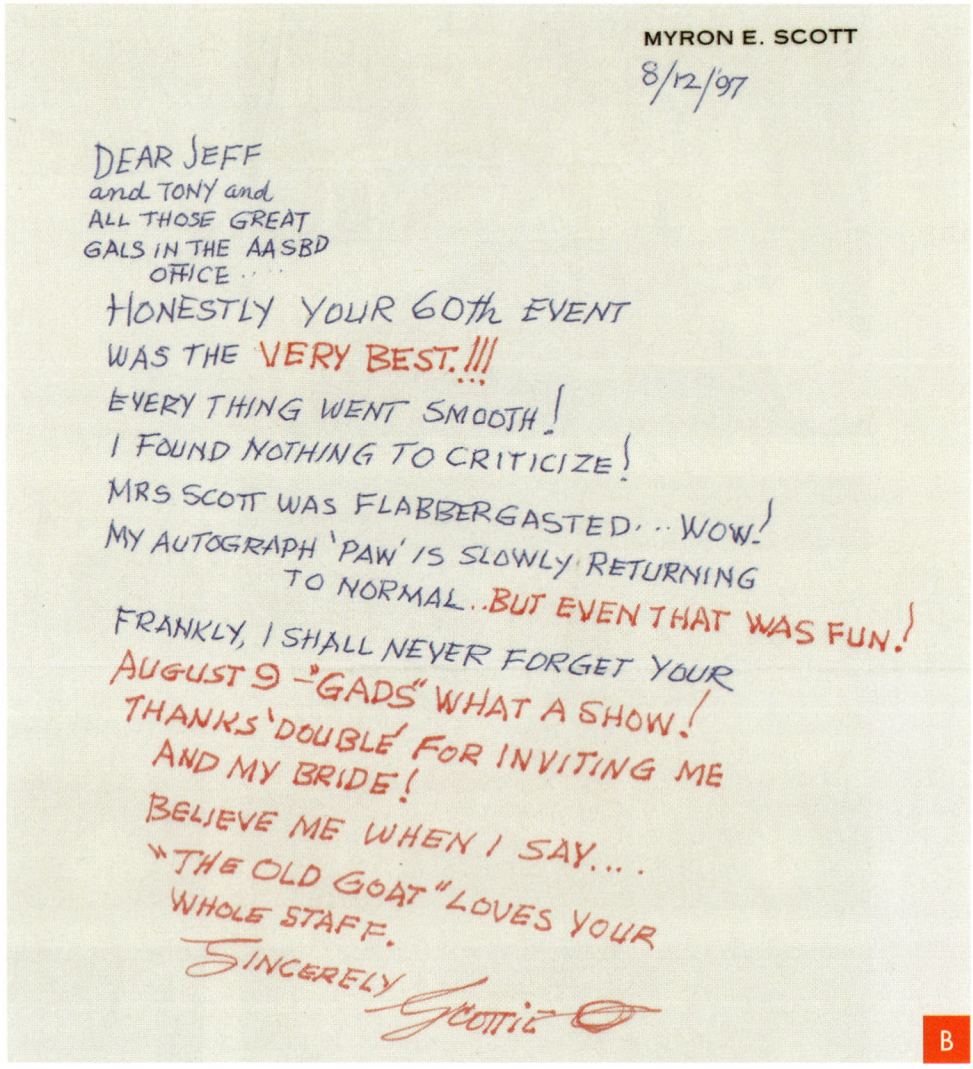

DEAR JEFF
and TONY and
ALL THOSE GREAT
GALS IN THE AASBD
OFFICE...
HONESTLY YOUR 60th EVENT
WAS THE VERY BEST.!!!
EVERY THING WENT SMOOTH!
I FOUND NOTHING TO CRITICIZE!
MRS SCOTT WAS FLABBERGASTED... WOW!
MY AUTOGRAPH 'PAW' IS SLOWLY RETURNING
     TO NORMAL...BUT EVEN THAT WAS FUN!
FRANKLY, I SHALL NEVER FORGET YOUR
AUGUST 9 - "GADS" WHAT A SHOW!
THANKS 'DOUBLE' FOR INVITING ME
AND MY BRIDE!
BELIEVE ME WHEN I SAY....
"THE OLD GOAT" LOVES YOUR
     WHOLE STAFF.
          SINCERELY
          Scottie

A Me (right) showing my dad, Ralph, my All-American Soap Box Derby Hall of Fame plaque. This was the last photo taken of my dad, who passed in November 2006

B Myron Scott, founder of the Derby, was invited to Akron in 1997 to be the first person inducted in the Derby Hall of Fame. He hadn't been to the race in 40 years, 1997

C Corbin Bernsen has collected over 7,000 snow globes. When I heard about his collection, I gave him my Soap Box Derby snow globe, a memento from a 1957 Akron, OH, local race, 2010

How I Saw It